MW00441662

Prayers for the Forgotten Single Expectant Mother

Natasha DeCruise

T&J PUBLISHERS

A SMALL INDEPENDENT PUBLISHER WITH A BIG VOICE

Printed in the United States of America by
T&J Publishers (Atlanta, GA.)
www.TandJPublishers.com

All scriptures used are from the People's Parallel Bible: KJV (King James Version)/NLT (New Living Translation), 2nd Edition created by Tyndale

Cover Design by Natasha DeCruise
Book Format/Layout by Timothy Flemming, Jr.

ISBN: 978-1-7345105-6-0

To contact the author, go to:
Email: Info@realwomenwhopray.com
Instagram: RealWomenWhoPray

Dedication

I dedicate this prayer book to my son Chase and unborn son Chauncey. I love you so much; I will bend over backward to ensure your every single need is met. The second-best decision I made in my life after following Jesus Christ was making the decision not to abort my children. I had my children out of wedlock, but God still held my hand and allowed me to deliver my kings with safety. While people counted me out, God never left me. I faced hardship, but by the grace of God, I overcame these challenges and am proud to say I am the mother of two handsome, mighty, brilliant, prosperous, athletic, holy children of God.

"Single moms: You are a doctor, a teacher, a nurse, a maid, a cook, a referee, a heroine, a provider, a defender, a protector, a true superwoman. Wear your cape proudly."- Mandy Hale

Table of Contents

Preface

I woke up one morning and realized there is plenty of literature on childbirth, pregnancy, and co-parenting, but what about a prayer book? While I was pregnant with my son Chase, I had to get a surgical procedure called a cerclage to stitch my cervix to avoid me losing another child due to preterm labor. I was in and out of the emergency room numerous times during that pregnancy; I even had to take pills to prevent me from going into preterm labor. All I knew to do was pray my way through, and with the help of God almost at 39 weeks, I delivered a 6-pound 15 oz healthy, beautiful, intelligent baby boy. It was a relive to hold my baby and see him face to face. Prayer is always my best friend during the good times and the bad times. Now at 18 weeks pregnant, I'm pregnant with another king I find myself feeling the same feelings I felt while pregnant with Chase. I decided to pray my way through and create a prayer book to help expectant mothers turn fear into faith. One last thing, before I say any prayer, I repent of all my sins and give God the praise and glory he deserves. Remember my beautiful child of God; there is nothing impossible for God (Luke 1:37 NLT).

Section One

Childbirth Fear

Prayer 1

Father God, I just want to thank you for being the one true living God. I came to the realization I am nothing without you. God, you made heaven and earth. I love you because you loved me first. I want to let you know God; you are the center of my life. I'm deciding this day forth I will trust you in this difficult time knowing that you will deliver me from all fears I have pertaining to this pregnancy. When I wake up every morning your face, I will seek, when I go to bed, your face I will seek. Lord, please remove all these fears out my life and ensure me my child will live and have a healthy, prosperous, holy, wealthy, world-changing lifestyle. God, please protect my child while he or she is in my womb. Heavenly Father, I ask you to keep my child and me from the terrors of the night and the arrow that flies in the day. I trust you, God, and I will walk by faith, knowing all of my fears have been removed and transformed into faith. Thank you, God, for being a supreme God and the God who answers by fire. I love you, Lord; in Jesus name, I pray amen.

Bible Verses

"In the beginning God created the heaven and the earth"
- Genesis 1:1 NLT

"We love him, because he first loved us" - 1 John 4: 19 KJV

"Because I am righteous, I will see you. When I awake, I will see you face to face and be satisfied." - Psalm 17:5 NLT

"Thou shalt not be afraid for the terror by night; nor for the arrow that flieth by day; 6 Nor for the pestilence that walketh in darkness; nor for the destruction that wasteth at noonday."
- Psalm 91: 5-6 KJV

"And call ye on the name of your gods, and I will call on the name of the LORD: and the God that answereth by fire, let him be God. And all the people answered and said, It is well spoken." - 1 Kings 18:24 KJV

Prayer 2

Oh God, here I come to you with fear on my mind. I feel defeated and unusable, but God, I know I am the apple of your eyes if It wasn't true you wouldn't have sent your only begotten son Jesus to die on the cross for me. Jesus came so that I can have everlasting life and not perish. God, you know how I conceived this child, I may have been sinning or married, but God you're with me as I deliver my healthy, brilliant, whole child of God. I dedicate my child to you, and I give you my heart, mind, and soul to keep. Lord, you told me not to be afraid or discouraged because you are with me wherever I go. Even if I made my bed in hell, you are with me. Just like David sought you and you delivered him from all his fears, I ask you to do the same for me. Lord, remove this fear I feel while carrying my child. Lord, you allowed me to conceive this child, which is another reason why I know you will erase childbirth fear out of my life. I love you God even when sometimes it seems like I'm drifting away forgive me oh God, you mean the world to me. In your son Jesus name, I pray amen.

Bible Verses

"Keep me as the apple of the eye, hide me under the shadow of thy wings," - Psalms 17:8 KJV

"For God so loved the world, that he gave his only begotten Son, that whosoever believeth in him should not perish, but have everlasting life." - John 3:16 KJV

"Have not I commanded thee? Be strong and of a good courage; be not afraid, neither be thou dismayed: for the Lord thy God is with thee whithersoever thou goest." - Joshua 1:9 KJV

"If I ascend up into heaven, thou art there: if I make my bed in hell, behold, thou art there." - Psalms 139:8 KJV

"I sought the Lord, and he heard me, and delivered me from all my fears." - Psalms 34:4 KJV

Prayer 3

Lord, I'm so grateful I can call, and you will answer. Time after time, you have made yourself real to me. I hear the birds chirping; I see the sun shining, I'm a living testimony you are real because you breathe your air into me and woke me up this morning. How can I forget about your grace and mercy? You show me new mercies every day. God, you don't need a hype man; it's nothing I'm saying you haven't heard before or know, but please allow me to come to you humbly and guilt-free. God speak to me and through me. Ease all the fear I'm feeling and remain by my side through my pregnancy and after my pregnancy. Lord, let me not worry about tomorrow because tomorrow will worry about itself. Lord, you told me, do not fear, for I have redeemed you; I have summoned you by name; you are mine. How wonderful it is to know I am yours, and nothing can separate me from the love of God. In your son's holy name Jesus, I pray amen.

Bible Verses

"It is of the Lord's mercies that we are not consumed, because his compassions fail not. They are new every morning: great is thy faithfulness." - Lamentations 3:22-23 KJV

"So, don't worry about tomorrow, for tomorrow will bring its own worries. Today's trouble is enough for today." - Matthew 6:34 NLT

"But now thus saith the Lord that created thee, O Jacob, and

he that formed thee, O Israel, Fear not: for I have redeemed thee, I have called thee by thy name; thou art mine."
- Isaiah 43:1 KJV

"For I am persuaded, that neither death, nor life, nor angels, nor principalities, nor powers, nor things present, nor things to come, Nor height, nor depth, nor any other creature, shall be able to separate us from the love of God, which is in Christ Jesus our Lord." - Romans 8:38-39 KJV

Prayer 4

Lord, I'm stopping by again to say you're a sovereign God who doesn't sleep nor slumber. How delighted I feel to know my God rules everything and takes no breaks. God, as fear tries to paralyze me, I rebuke and cancel out all forms of doubt in my life. I don't care how fear sneaked in my life, but with you, I know fear has no power. You have given me the power to tread on serpents and scorpions, and over all the power of the enemy: and nothing shall by any means hurt me. Thank you, God, I fear you and no one else. By fearing you, God, I depart from evil. God with you, I'm powerful, but without you, I'm powerless. Thank you, God, for your daily blessings and unconditional love In Jesus name I pray amen.

Bible Verses

"Behold, he that keepeth Israel shall neither slumber nor sleep." - Psalms 121:4 KJV

"Behold, I give unto you power to tread on serpents and scorpions, and over all the power of the enemy: and nothing shall by any means hurt you." - Luke 10:19 KJV

"By mercy and truth iniquity is purged: and by the fear of the Lord men depart from evil." - Proverbs 16:6 KJV

Prayer 5

God, today, I'm feeling dull like I'm facing this pregnancy all by myself. No, I haven't done everything right or lived my life identical to Christ, but I believe you're a God that is married to the backslider. God, you are waiting to hear my voice and want me to spend time with you. If I only draw near to you, God, you said you would draw near to me. Please draw near to me; don't leave me out in this cold world where abortions are common, and pregnancy complications are at its peak. God, you know how my child got here; you know if it was on purpose or a mistake, but forgive me for any negative feelings, thoughts, or words I had toward my unborn child. You give life and take a life; it is only through you; I conceived this child I am carrying. Thank you, God, for being concerned about me, you will leave the 99 sheep to look for me the lost sheep. God, you are magnificent and worth calling my father, master, and everything. In the matchless name of Jesus, I pray amen.

Bible Verses

"Turn, O backsliding children, saith the Lord; for I am married unto you: and I will take you one of a city, and two of a family, and I will bring you to Zion:" - Jeremiah 3:14 KJV

"Draw nigh to God, and he will draw nigh to you. Cleanse your hands, ye sinners; and purify your hearts, ye double minded." - James 4:8 KJV

"The Lord gives both death and life; he brings some down to the grave but raises others up." - 1 Samuel 2:6 NLT

"How think ye? if a man have an hundred sheep, and one of them be gone astray, doth he not leave the ninety and nine, and goeth into the mountains, and seeketh that which is gone astray?" - Matthew 18:12 KJV

Prayer 6

As your daughter God I just want to tell you my concerns and my fear during this pregnancy. I'm casting all my cares on you for you care for me. I don't know what scares me more, delivering the baby, or being a mother to my baby. Lord, prepare me to love this child the way you intended parents to love their children. Clothe me with extra strength so I can deliver this baby with or without medicine. Thank you, Jesus, I am free from sickness and diseases. I'm healthy, and my child is healthy. My faith today, Lord, is making me whole and free from all fears, depressions, and disorders. I ask you that my child obeys me, and I don't provoke my child. My child and I will have a beautiful, holy bond without confusion, sorrow, and disrespect. God, please supply my every need, so I am in a predicament I always provide for my child and me nor my child will know what it means or feels like to struggle. Please show me the way that leads me to being a great mother who is attentive to their child's every need. I will support my child, but I will also correct my child when necessary. Thank you for loving my child and loving me in Jesus name I pray amen.

Bible Verses

"Casting all your care upon him; for he careth for you."
- 1 Peter 5:7 KJV

"Honor your father and mother." This is the first commandment with a promise." - Ephesians 6:2 NLT

"Fathers do not provoke your children to anger by the way you treat them. Rather, bring them up with the discipline and instruction that comes from the Lord." - Ephesians 6:4 NLT

"But my God shall supply all your need according to his riches in glory by Christ Jesus." - Philippians 4:19 KJV

Prayer 7

Jesus, Jesus, Jesus, how sweet is your holy name. Who can compare to you? You are the son of God who walked this earth was tempted but did not sin. You died on the cross for me, and I know that was complex, but Jesus, I ask that I have the same mind you have. I want to walk like you, talk like you, pray like you, do everything like you. Show me, God, how to be like you. I'm crucifying my flesh daily because the spirit is indeed willing, but my flesh is weak. Make me over Lord pour your spirit out on me so my child can prophesy, and we see visions and have dreams. Let your vast arms protect my unborn child and me in your arms; we are perfectly safe. I adore you and want to please you. I don't just want you to remove my fear and anxiety. I want you to make me over into the women you predestined me to be. I love you Heavenly Father in your son Jesus name I pray amen.

Bible Verses

"For we have not an high priest which cannot be touched with the feeling of our infirmities; but was in all points tempted like as we are, yet without sin." - Hebrews 4:15 KJV

"And they that are Christ's have crucified the flesh with the affections and lusts." - Galatians 5:24 KJV

"Watch and pray, that ye enter not into temptation: the spirit indeed is willing, but the flesh is weak." - Matthew 26:41 KJV

"And it shall come to pass in the last days, saith God, I will pour out of my Spirit upon all flesh: and your sons and your daughters shall prophesy, and your young men shall see visions, and your old men shall dream dreams:" - Acts 2:17 KJV

*"He shall cover thee with his feathers, and under his wings shalt thou trust: his truth shall be thy shield and buckler."
- Psalm 91:4 KJV*

Prayer 8

Lover of my soul, I come humbly before you with thanksgiving in my heart and praise in me. The doctors and specialists consider me high risk, but God, your word says heal me oh lord I am healed save me oh lord I am saved. God, I'm declaring and decreeing right now my unborn child and I are covered with the blood of Jesus from the crown of our head to the sores of our feet. This fear that is in me is not from you or of you. God continue to show me you are real by the daily blessings I receive every day. Right now, I'm putting the full armor of God on and allowing you to fight this battle of fear in my life. Fear will not affect my unborn child or me because I defeated fear with the blood of Jesus. I'm so thankful you answer when I call. I love you God and think the world of you in Jesus name I pray amen.

Bible Verses

"Enter his gates with thanksgiving; go into his courts with praise. Give thanks to him and praise his name." - Psalms 100:4 NLT

"O Lord, if you heal me, I will be truly healed; if you save me, I will be truly saved. My praises are for you alone!" - Jeremiah 17:14 NLT

"Wherefore take unto you the whole armour of God, that ye may be able to withstand in the evil day, and having done all, to stand." - Ephesians 6:13 KJV

Prayer 9

In the midst of me fearing to deliver this baby, you are with me even to the ends of the earth. Childbearing comes with pain and nurturing I want to be the best mother to my child. God don't allow me to be a mother who stresses herself out and forfeit being a mother. You told Adam and Eve to be fruitful and multiply having children is a part of the deal. I know you got my back regardless of what I see with my natural eyes. God, sometimes it's so hard to walk by faith and not by sight. Forty weeks of carrying life is a task you felt I was fit for. You bless me with this child and will see me through. Lord, I ask that you give me a new mindset and wash away my old mindset filled with fear. You stop generational curses; just because it happened to other women in my family does not mean it will happen to me. Lord, because of you, I am going to remain steadfast on your word and pray my way through this entire pregnancy. Lord, I know you are with me. I will not be afraid. I will continue to press in your presence; I love you God and bless your holy name. In Jesus name, I pray amen.

Bible Verses

"To the woman He said, "I will greatly multiply Your pain in childbirth, in pain you will bring forth children; Yet your desire will be for your husband, and he will rule over you." - Genesis 3:16 KJV

"Then God blessed them and said, "Be fruitful and multiply. Fill the earth and govern it. Reign over the fish in the sea,

the birds in the sky, and all the animals that scurry along the ground." - Genesis 1:28 NLT

"For we walk by faith, not by sight." - 2 Corinthans 5:7 KJV

"The LORD is on my side; I will not fear. What can man do to me?" - Psalm 118:6 KJV

Prayer 10

Lord, thank you for being my help and shield. Shield me from this thing called fear. Fear is beneath you, and because I am your child, I am joint-heirs with Christ, meaning fear is beneath me too. I have all the time in the world to exalt you. Jehovah Shammah, you are always present. I feel security and protection when I talk to you. Lord I desire a real relationship with you where I spend so much time caught up in your presence, I have no time in the world. The love you have for me, I can't find anywhere else. Love is fearless; perfect love drives out fear. Your love is pure and perfect, which is why you will and have freed me from all my fears. Many nights I cried, but knowing weeping last through the night, but joy comes in the morning increases my faith. You keep track of all my sorrows and collect my tears in your bottle. A human can uplift me and encourage me, but you have the power to change me. Oh God, thank you for changing me. I love the way you continuously love me and protect me. I am trusting in you believing the chains of fear is broken and will never appear again. Help me to pray your perfect will over my life in the miracle-working name of Jesus I pray amen.

Bible Verses

"We put our hope in the LORD. He is our help and our shield."
- Psalm 33:20 NLT

"And if children, then heirs; heirs of God, and joint heirs with Christ; if so be that we suffer with him, that we may be also

glorified together." - Romans 8:17 KJV

"For his anger lasts only a moment, but his favor lasts a lifetime! Weeping may last through the night, but joy comes with the morning." - Psalm 30:5 NLT

"There is no fear in love; but perfect love casteth out fear: because fear hath torment. He that feareth is not made perfect in love." - 1 John 4:18 KJV

Prayer 11

God, you haven't given me a spirit of fear but of power love and of a sound mind. I ask you right now to drive fear out of every part of my life. Fear is not of you; it's of the devil. The only one my child and I will fear is you father God the Holy and true One. Thank you God I don't have an anxious heart that's weighing me down, but I continue to say kind words that will cheer me and others up. Lord, I speak your word over me and my unborn child's life you will come and save us. Fear is a feeling that I have no desire to have. I'm carrying my unborn child with no fears because Lord, you are my portion; therefore, I will hope in you. Let your mercy, O Lord, be upon us, accordingly, as we (me and my unborn child) hope in thee. In the one true Messiah Jesus name, I pray amen.

Bible Verses

"For God hath not given us the spirit of fear; but of power, and of love, and of a sound mind." - 2 Timothy 1:7 KJV

"I am the Lord, your Holy One, the creator of Israel, your King." - Isaiah 43:15 KJV

"Worry weighs a person down; an encouraging word cheers a person up." - Proverbs 12:25 NLT

"Say to those with fearful hearts, "Be strong, and do not fear, for your God is coming to destroy your enemies. He is coming to save you." - Isaiah 35:4 NLT

"The Lord is my portion, saith my soul; therefore, will I hope in him." - Lamentations 3:24 KJV

Prayer 12

Lord, you are my light and salvation whom shall, I fear? I have no reason to doubt you have delivered me from fear, Lord; you are the only deliverer I know. A psychologist can't deliver me; no medicine can deliver me, not even witchcraft. Lord, forgive me if I have unknowingly practiced sorcery and open a door for Satan. I am resisting Satan, and he has no choice but to flee because the word of God is quick, powerful, and sharper than any two-edged sword. God, you know if the physicians working on my body is evil or good. If they are doers of evil, stop me from receiving services from them and lead me to the physicians who are anointed and called by you to assist me in my pregnancy. I rebuke every witch and warlock hiding behind a medical degree and certificate in the mighty name of Jesus I pray amen.

Bible Verses

"The Lord is my light and my salvation— so why should I be afraid? The Lord is my fortress, protecting me from danger, so why should I tremble?" - Psalms 27:1 NLT

"And he said, The Lord is my rock, and my fortress, and my deliverer" - 2 Samuel 22:2 KJV

"Submit yourselves therefore to God. Resist the devil, and he will flee from you." - James 4:7 KJV

"For the word of God is quick, and powerful, and sharper

than any two-edged sword, piercing even to the dividing asunder of soul and spirit, and of the joints and marrow, and is a discerner of the thoughts and intents of the heart." - Hebrews 4:12 KJV

Prayer 13

God forgive me for the mornings and the nights I forget to reverence your holy name. Your name is above all names. I always come to you with a problem, but you are the problem solver. All the glory and dominion belong to you forever and ever. It was your will; I am the mother of my unborn child as you form my baby in my womb. I know you got me and my child's best interest. God, your word said your strength is made perfect in weakness. How good it is to know in my weakest moments you are right there doing a good work in me. It's so easy to be consumed with this world to the point I forget that everything belongs to you. Jesus stay close to me as I am faced with a life-changing decision called pregnancy. Doctors only practice medicine, but you are the ultimate healer the balm in Gilead. When Mary brother Lazarus was announced dead and Mary thought Jesus was too late on the fourth day, Jesus raised Lazarus from the dead. God, you are never a day late, or a dollar short your always right on time. God, I am fearing you and only you in Jesus name I pray amen.

Bible Verses

"Wherefore God also hath highly exalted him, and given him a name which is above every name" - Philippians 2:9 KJV

"Thine, O Lord, is the greatness, and the power, and the glory, and the victory, and the majesty: for all that is in the heaven and in the earth is thine; thine is the kingdom, O Lord, and

thou art exalted as head above all." - 1 Chronicles 29:11 KJV

"And he said unto me, my grace is sufficient for thee: for my strength is made perfect in weakness. Most gladly therefore will I rather glory in my infirmities, that the power of Christ may rest upon me." - 2 Corinthians 12:9 KJV

"Is there no balm in Gilead; is there no physician there? why then is not the health of the daughter of my people recovered?" - Jeremiah 8:22 KJV

"Then when Jesus came, he found that he had lain in the grave four days already." - John 11:17 KJV

"But, beloved, be not ignorant of this one thing, that one day is with the Lord as a thousand years, and a thousand years as one day." - 2 Peter 3:8 KJV

Prayer 14

Greetings God, I'm excited to say the more I pray to you about fear and read your word, I feel one hundred percent free from all worries. I was upside down when I first came to you, but now Lord, I'm on my guard, stand firm on my faith, feel courageous, and strong. I feel like a brand-new person I feel like David when he defeated Goliath, the giant. God provide the tools for me to triumph over fear. Equip me to stay fearless in this pregnancy. Lord, when I feel anxious or doubtful, bring Bible verses to mind that reminds me, you're the God that answers by fire, and you answer prayers of your righteous people. Lord, your word will not return void. I know if you spoke it over my child and me, it would come to pass. Gideon was filled with fear, but you used him and three hundred men to defeat the Midianites. God, you did it for Gideon, who was the least of his family, so I know you can do it for me because you are the same God today, yesterday, and forevermore. Thank you for being the God who is true and real I love you in your son Jesus name I pray amen.

Bible Verses

"Be on guard. Stand firm in the faith. Be courageous. Be strong." - 1 Corinthians 16:13 NLT

"So, David triumphed over the Philistine with only a sling and a stone, for he had no sword." - 1 Samuel 17:50 NLT

"And call ye on the name of your gods, and I will call on

the name of the Lord: and the God that answereth by fire, let him be God. And all the people answered and said, it is well spoken." - 1 Kings 18:24 KJV

"The Lord is far from the wicked: but he heareth the prayer of the righteous." - Proverbs 15:29 KJV

"So shall my word be that goeth forth out of my mouth: it shall not return unto me void, but it shall accomplish that which I please, and it shall prosper in the thing whereto I sent it." - Isaiah 55:11 KJV

"When the 300 Israelites blew their rams' horns, the Lord caused the warriors in the camp to fight against each other with their swords. Those who were not killed fled to places as far away as Beth-shittah near Zererah and to the border of Abel-meholah near Tabbath." - Judges 7:22 NLT

"Jesus Christ is the same yesterday, today, and forever." - Hebrews 13:8 NLT

Chapter Two

Loss Of A Child

Prayer 15

Lord, my heart is beating fast; I do not know if I feel sad or happy. Once again, I am pregnant, but God, you know how much I suffered from my last pregnancy. I conceived, but my child is not living; my child is with you instead of me. God, I ask you that I never lose another child again. I desire to keep this child in my womb full term without birth effects, abnormalities, disabilities, chromosome issues, and disorders. Please turn my mourning into joyful dancing. Take away my clothes of mourning and clothe me with joy. I am done with mourning now is the time you comfort me. God grant my petition as you granted Hanna's petition and bless me with a child. Lord, you knew my child before you formed him/her in my womb. Before my child is born, you set my child apart and appointed my child as a prophet to the nations. I am not gone worry about anything, but in everything by prayer and supplication with thanksgiving, let my request be known to you, God. If Sarah conceived through faith and delivered her baby, Lord help me to increase my faith as well. God do the unexpected in this pregnancy wow me and blow my mind. Show doctors why the Israelites know you to be Lord the Healer. I am praising you and thanking you in advance for blessing me with a healthy, beautiful, brilliant, infirmity free baby who will surpass me in years. In the matchless name of Jesus, I pray amen.

Bible Verses

"You have turned my mourning into joyful dancing.

41

You have taken away my clothes of mourning and clothed me with joy," - Psalm 30:11 NLT

"God blesses those who mourn, for they will be comforted." - Matthew 5:4 NLT

"Wherefore it came to pass, when the time was come about after Hannah had conceived, that she bare a son, and called his name Samuel, saying, Because I have asked him of the Lord." - 1 Samuel 1:20

"I knew you before I formed you in your mother's womb. Before you were born, I set you apart and appointed you as my prophet to the nations." - Jeremiah 1:5 NLT

"Don't worry about anything; instead, pray about everything. Tell God what you need and thank him for all he has done." - Philippians 4:6 NLT

"It was by faith that even Sarah was able to have a child, though she was barren and was too old. She believed that God would keep his promise." - Hebrews 11:11 NLT

"And said, If thou wilt diligently hearken to the voice of the Lord thy God, and wilt do that which is right in his sight, and wilt give ear to his commandments, and keep all his statutes, I will put none of these diseases upon thee, which I have brought upon the Egyptians: for I am the Lord that healeth thee." - Exodus 15:26 KJV

"Devote yourselves to prayer with an alert mind and a thankful heart." - Colossians 4:2 NLT

Prayer 16

Lord, you are my only option. A doctor didn't help me conceive or can control the outcome of my pregnancy. Lord, show me how powerful you are and continue to breathe life into my child. Lord, let this baby's body form entirely without any missing limbs. The doctor said I need a cerclage, but Lord, you are my cerclage you are keeping my baby safely in my womb. Lord, I know that you will guarantee I have a full-term healthy pregnancy because you are the God that heals. The last pregnancy wasn't what I expected, but this present pregnancy will be better than my past pregnancy. God, you are the only one who knows why my last pregnancy was a struggle, but whatever attack Satan has sent my way, God expose it and dismantle it right now with your power. Jesus, you came to destroy the works of Satan, so I ask you right now to destroy them immediately. Lord, you are the God of peace; thank you for crushing Satan under your feet. Every human and spirit working for Satan God send your wrath to deliver them in my hands in Jesus Holy name I pray amen.

Bible Verses

"And the Lord God formed man of the dust of the ground and breathed into his nostrils the breath of life; and man became a living soul." - Genesis 2:7 KJV

"But he was pierced for our rebellion, crushed for our sins. He was beaten so we could be whole. He was whipped so we could be healed." - Isaiah 53:5 NLT

"The future glory of this Temple will be greater than its past glory, says the LORD of Heaven's Armies. And in this place, I will bring peace. I, the LORD of Heaven's Armies, have spoken!" - Haggai 2:9 NLT

*"He that committeth sin is of the devil; for the devil sinneth from the beginning. For this purpose, the Son of God was manifested, that he might destroy the works of the devil."
- 1 John 3:8 KJV*

"The God of peace will soon crush Satan under your feet. May the grace of our Lord Jesus be with you." - Romans 16:20 NLT

"Then said Abishai to David, God hath delivered thine enemy into thine hand this day: now therefore let me smite him, I pray thee, with the spear even to the earth at once, and I will not smite him the second time." - 1 Samuel 26:8 KJV

Prayer 17

Lord, I want to take time out of my schedule and tell you how much I need and want you. God, some consider me barren, but God, you open the womb of the barren, and there will be no miscarriages or infertility in my land. The fruit of my womb is blessed, yes, Lord, you blessed my baby. Lord, help me to keep my mind stayed on you because if I do, then you will keep me in perfect peace. Jesus, you are the prince of peace and desire me to live in peace. I know I cannot conceive or deliver this healthy baby without your help. I ask you, Lord, to remove all negative thoughts and flashbacks from my previous pregnancies, you told me not to dwell in the past, so I won't. I will not be like Lot's wife and turn into a pillar of salt. I don't care what statistics say only what you say matters. God, just like you did for Daniel, I ask you to shut the lion's mouth; don't allow any negative words to be heard in my ears father God. Jesus, you're so perfect, and your name is sweet. God, the barren woman in the Bible such as Sarah, Rebekah, Rachel, Hannah, Elisabeth, and Manoah's wife, conceived and delivered powerful, mighty men of God. Some of these men are trailblazers to our faith. God, I just know you got the best in-stored for my child and me. I can't wait to see how my unborn child turns out and be exactly what my child was predestined to be by you God in Jesus name I pray amen.

Bible Verses

"There will be no miscarriages or infertility in your land, and I

will give you long, full lives." - *Exodus 23:26 NLT*

"And she spake out with a loud voice, and said, blessed art thou among women, and blessed is the fruit of thy womb." - *Luke 1:42 KJV*

"Thou wilt keep him in perfect peace, whose mind is stayed on thee: because he trusteth in thee." - *Isaiah 26:3 KJV*

"For unto us a child is born, unto us a son is given, and the government shall be upon his shoulder: and his name shall be called Wonderful, Counsellor, The mighty God, The everlasting Father, The Prince of Peace." - *Isaiah 9:6 KJV*

"Remember ye not the former things, neither consider the things of old." - *Isaiah 43:18 KJV*

"But his wife looked back from behind him, and she became a pillar of salt." - *Genesis 19:26 KJV*

"My God hath sent his angel, and hath shut the lions' mouths, that they have not hurt me: forasmuch as before him innocency was found in me; and also, before thee, O king, have I done no hurt." - *Daniel 6:22 KJV*

"And being made perfect, he became the author of eternal salvation unto all them that obey him;" - *Hebrews 5:9 KJV*

"For Sarah conceived, and bare Abraham a son in his old age, at the set time of which God had spoken to him." - *Genesis 21:2 KJV*

"And Isaac entreated the Lord for his wife, because she was barren: and the Lord was entreated of him, and Rebekah his

wife conceived." - *Genesis 25:21 KJV*

"*And God remembered Rachel, and God hearkened to her, and opened her womb. And she conceived, and bare a son; and said, God hath taken away my reproach:*" - *Genesis 30:22-23 KJV*

"*And, behold, thy cousin Elisabeth, she hath also conceived a son in her old age: and this is the sixth month with her, who was called barren.*" - *Luke 1:36 KJV*

"*And there was a certain man of Zorah, of the family of the Danites, whose name was Manoah; and his wife was barren, and bare not. And the angel of the Lord appeared unto the woman, and said unto her, behold now, thou art barren, and bearest not: but thou shalt conceive, and bear a son.*"
- Judges 13:2-3 KJV

Prayer 18

God losing a child makes a person feel inadequate, how can a person with no health conditions lose a child? Lord, my blood work was excellent, my size was perfect, and my baby was growing healthy day by day. How could this happen to me? Why me, but then again Lord, why not me? Jesus died for the whole humanity; he lost it all just so I can be free from sin. Losing a child is another chapter added to my story. I know I overcome by the blood of the lamb and every word of my testimony. God, it felt like I walked in the hall of shame after everyone found out I lost my child. People were insensitive, asking me for full details of the loss of my child. God, I don't need sympathy; I need your compassion. God, just touch me and restore me. Please give me a fresh start and a new beginning. God, you don't look at our outward appearance; you look at our hearts. Lord, you can tell from my heart I yearn to continue to carry this child in my womb full term without any pregnancy complications. You are the great physician; no one will die on your clock if it's not your will. Satan is defeated, Jesus bruised your head, so you're under my feet. God continue to expose Satan and all his counterfeit ways in Jesus sweet and perfect name I pray amen.

Bible Verses

"And that he died for all, that they which live should not henceforth live unto themselves, but unto him which died for them, and rose again." - 2 Corinthians 5:15 KJV

"And they overcame him by the blood of the Lamb, and by the word of their testimony; and they loved not their lives unto the death." - Revelation 12:11 KJV

"The Lord is gracious, and full of compassion; slow to anger, and of great mercy." - Psalms 145:8 KJV

"For your shame ye shall have double; and for confusion they shall rejoice in their portion: therefore, in their land they shall possess the double: everlasting joy shall be unto them." - Isaiah 61:7 KJV

"But the Lord said unto Samuel, look not on his countenance, or on the height of his stature; because I have refused him: for the Lord seeth not as man seeth; for man looketh on the outward appearance, but the Lord looketh on the heart." - 1 Samuel 16:7 KJV

"And I will put enmity between thee and the woman, and between thy seed and her seed; it shall bruise thy head, and thou shalt bruise his heel." - Genesis 3:15 KJV

Prayer 19

Lord, I sit here with distraught because losing a child seems like a horror movie. I can remember my water breaking and my contractions kicking in. The doctor is telling me it's a 50/50 chance my baby lives. My blood pressure is high, and I feel like I'm losing my mind. Lord, where did I go wrong? I lost so much blood, I feel like I'm half past dead. Nothing the doctor, my family, or friends are saying is consoling. God, I prayed and prayed before my delivery and during my delivery, and still, my baby is dead. God, I want to make up my mind that this pregnancy is different, and my body will not give out on me. David and Bathsheba lost their first child, but David didn't curse you; he went into the Lord's house to worship you. God don't let me fall into Satan trap of depression, but let me hope in you and not be put to shame because your love has been poured out into my heart. Many think trying again is a bad idea, but God, you are my shield around me, my glory, the one who lifts my head high. When times get tough, God talk to me and tell me everything will be okay. Your word says there are more on my side than on theirs! I know you can answer this prayer and all of the prayers above. Thank you, God, for expediting the answers to my prayer. I love you and adore you, God, in that matchless name of Jesus I pray amen.

Bible Verses

"Then David arose from the earth, and washed, and anointed

himself, and changed his apparel, and came into the house of the Lord, and worshipped: then he came to his own house; and when he required, they set bread before him, and he did eat." - 2 Samuel 12:20 KJV

"And hope maketh not ashamed; because the love of God is shed abroad in our hearts by the Holy Ghost which is given unto us." - Romans 5:5 KJV

"But you, O Lord, are a shield around me; you are my glory, the one who holds my head high." - Psalms 3:3 NLT

" 'Don't be afraid!' Elisha told him. 'For there are more on our side than on theirs!'" - 2 Kings 6:16 NLT

Prayer 20

Heavenly Father, you're so amazing and love everything about me flaws and all. Jesus, you're a friend that sticks closer than a brother, you're my dearest closes friend. Holy Spirit, you descended from the heavens, and you are an excellent comforter. I'm grateful for the gifts and fruits of the spirit you give me. God, because of you, I got Jesus who is with me even until the ends of the earth I got the Holy Spirit who gives me power. I can't make it on my own and need your guidance through this pregnancy. I'm called according to your purpose, and I love you, so I know this pregnancy is worked out in my favor. My present suffering is not worth comparing to the glory that will be revealed to me. Thank you, God, for this child or children in my womb that will live and not die. God give my body the power and strength to finish this pregnancy with the results I'm expecting. It's nothing too hard for you; God with you, I know my pregnancy is in your hands. I love you, Lord, always and forever in Jesus name I pray amen.

Bible Verses

"A man that hath friends must shew himself friendly: and there is a friend that sticketh closer than a brother." - Proverbs 18:24 KJV

"And I will pray the Father, and he shall give you another Comforter, that he may abide with you forever;" - John 14:16 KJV

"Now there are diversities of gifts, but the same Spirit."
- 1 Corinthians 12:4 KJV

"But the fruit of the Spirit is love, joy, peace, longsuffering, gentleness, goodness, faith, Meekness, temperance: against such there is no law." - Galatians 5:22-23 KJV

"Teaching them to observe all things whatsoever I have commanded you: and, lo, I am with you alway, even unto the end of the world. Amen." - Matthew 28:20 KJV

"And we know that all things work together for good to them that love God, to them who are the called according to his purpose." - Romans 8:28 KJV

"For I reckon that the sufferings of this present time are not worthy to be compared with the glory which shall be revealed in us." - Romans 8:18 KJV

"I shall not die, but live, and declare the works of the Lord." - Psalms 118:17 KJV

"Behold, I am the Lord, the God of all flesh: is there anything too hard for me?" - Jeremiah 32:27 KJV

Prayer 21

God prepare my body to give birth to my child. Dismantle every ungodly thought I have about delivering my child. Help me father God to consider it pure joy when I face a trial in my pregnancy. Lord, I know you take delight in my gladness, so I request that I remain joyful through this pregnancy. I obeyed your commandment when I decided not to have an abortion. Instead of aborting my child, I look to you, Jesus. God, I know you have the power to turn any situation around. I believe in your word that no one will be able to stand against me. Satan himself can't stand against me in this pregnancy. I cast down imaginations and every high thing that exalts itself against the knowledge of God. God give me the words to say during my pregnancy; let me speak kind words that are like honey. Stop my mouth God from speaking anything evil that will block you from answering my prayers in Jesus Holy name I pray amen.

Bible Verses

"Dear brothers and sisters, when troubles of any kind come your way, consider it an opportunity for great joy. For you know that when your faith is tested, your endurance has a chance to grow." - James 1:2-3 NLT

"For the Lord your God is living among you. He is a mighty savior. He will take delight in you with gladness. With his love, he will calm all your fears. He will rejoice over you with joyful songs." - Zephaniah 3:17 NLT

"No one will be able to stand against you, for the Lord your God will cause the people to fear and dread you, as he promised, wherever you go in the whole land." - Deuteronomy 11:25 NLT

"Casting down imaginations, and every high thing that exalteth itself against the knowledge of God, and bringing into captivity every thought to the obedience of Christ;"
- 2 Corinthians 10:5 KJV

"Pleasant words are as an honeycomb, sweet to the soul, and health to the bones." - Proverbs 16:24 KJV

Prayer 22

Lord, I can't help but think about your sovereignty, how time after time you forgave me of my sins. God, I can't express my gratitude and love for you. I'm pouring out my heart to you with tears in my eyes because I know you to be a God who performs miracles. You're not a lower-case false god, but you're the uppercase God who makes all things possible. Jesus, you turned water into wine, fed five thousand with five loaves of bread and two fish. No one can tell me that you can't form this baby into pure perfection. It doesn't matter what the blood work looks like or ultrasound all that matters is the work of your hands' father. I read about the lame walking and the blind seeing, so how much more can you do for my baby in my womb? My child didn't ask to be here, but as the mother of my unborn child, I'm asking you to take full control of my womb. I dedicate my baby to you; she belongs to you. Just like Hanna dedicated Samuel to you, I'm doing the same with my child. Lord, you know every hair on my baby's head, you know what you called my child to do on this earth. I ask you, God, to continue to breathe life into my child and mold my baby in your image in Jesus' name I pray amen.

Bible Verses

"But our God is in the heavens: he hath done whatsoever he hath pleased." - Psalms 115:3 KJV

"But Jesus beheld them, and said unto them, with men this is impossible; but with God all things are possible."

- Matthew 19:26 KJV

"And he commanded the multitude to sit down on the grass, and took the five loaves, and the two fishes, and looking up to heaven, he blessed, and brake, and gave the loaves to his disciples, and the disciples to the multitude. And they did all eat and were filled: and they took up of the fragments that remained twelve baskets full. And they that had eaten were about five thousand men, beside women and children." -
Matthew 14:19-21 KJV

"Jesus saith unto him, Rise, take up thy bed, and walk. And immediately the man was made whole, and took up his bed, and walked: and on the same day was the sabbath."
- John 5:8-9 KJV

"Then touched he their eyes, saying, according to your faith be it unto you. And their eyes were opened; and Jesus straitly charged them, saying, see that no man know it."
- Matthew 9:29-30 KJV

"But Hannah did not go. She told her husband, "Wait until the boy is weaned. Then I will take him to the Tabernacle and leave him there with the Lord permanently." - 1 Samuel 1:22 NLT

"And the very hairs on your head are all numbered." -
Matthew 10:30 NLT

"So, God created human beings in his own image. In the image of God, he created them; male and female he created them." -
Genesis 1:27 NLT

Prayer 23

I'm so tired of the doctor prescribing me medication and giving me Makena shots. Lord, I know I lost a child before, but God, I'm asking for a normal healthy pregnancy. A pregnancy where I don't have to go to the doctor weekly or see a high-risk specialist. Father God remove me out of the high-risk category and make everything about me whole. I'm thanking you now, Lord, for doing a new thing in me. It is you God who blessed me with my unborn child, every good and perfect gift is from above. I believe my baby is a perfect gift you have blessed me with. Lord, you are unchanging, if you helped women deliver babies in the Bible time, I know you can do it right now for me in this century. Everything you do endure forever, so God, please allow me to have a full-term pregnancy, raise and nurture my child until you call me to be with you in Jesus' name, I pray amen.

Bible Verses

"Behold, I will do a new thing; now it shall spring forth; shall ye not know it? I will even make a way in the wilderness, and rivers in the desert." - Isaiah 43:19 KJV

"Every good gift and every perfect gift is from above, and cometh down from the Father of lights, with whom is no variableness, neither shadow of turning." - James 1:17 KJV

"For I am the Lord, I change not; therefore, ye sons of Jacob are not consumed." - Malachi 3:6 KJV

"And I know that whatever God does is final. Nothing can be added to it or taken from it. God's purpose is that people should fear him." - Ecclesiastes 3:14 NLT

Prayer 24

Lion of Judah thank you for being my protector and crowning me with glory. Lord I need your glory to follow me everywhere I go. Just like Moses if your presence isn't with me God don't bring me up from here. God you knew exactly why I lost my child or children in the past. It may have been due to miscarriage, abortion, still birth, preterm labor, Sudden infant death syndrome (SIDS), or neonatal death. Whatever the cause Holy Spirit please intercept all forms of death that will try to attach itself to my child or children. I rebuke every spirit that is not of God that was sent from the father of lies to snatch the life out of my children. Satan comes to steal, kill, and destroy not you father God you want me have life and have it more abundantly. The screech owl also knows as Lilith the night demon is not welcome in my home or has any authority over my children. I rebuke the screech owl right now in Jesus name, Lord I ask that my angels hold the screech owl hostage and snatch the life out this demonic spirit that preys on children. God stop my enemies in their foot tracks, the pit they have dug for me they have fell in the pit themselves. God thank you for being just so good to me when I don't deserve it. I'm so grateful vengeances belong to you and not me. You will take care of me and you always deal with my enemies accordingly. I love you Lord and I won't place anyone above you in Jesus perfect name I pray amen.

Bible Verses

"And when the Great Shepherd appears, you will receive a

crown of never-ending glory and honor." - 1 Peter 5:4 NLT

"Then Moses said, "If you don't personally go with us, don't make us leave this place." - Exodus 33:15 NLT

"The thief cometh not, but for to steal, and to kill, and to destroy I am come that they might have life, and that they might have it more abundantly." - John 10:10 KJV

"They have prepared a net for my steps; my soul is bowed down: they have digged a pit before me, into the midst whereof they are fallen themselves. Selah." - Psalms 57:6 KJV

Prayers for the Forgotten Single Expectant Mother

Chapter Three

Single Mother

Prayer 25

Lord being a single mother isn't a joke, it seems overwhelming at times. Adding another child to my household brings me stress sometimes. I don't want to struggle with kids or live in an apartment all my life. I desire my kids to have the best: a home with a backyard. I want to feel comfortable when my kids play outside not worrying about stray bullets, hit and run, or sexual predators. Lord I know you won't give me more than I can bare you saw me fit to be the mother of my child or children. God if the father doesn't step up or if a man doesn't come soon, I pray and ask that you still provide all my needs according to your riches and glory. God keep food on my table, groceries in my fridge, gas in my car, shelter over our heads, clothes on our back, shoes on our feet and all our expenses paid. Father God provide my needs and wants I don't want to be the mother who does the minimum I want to do the maximum. God you won't abandon us because you made us. Provide for me Lord the same way you provided the Israelites with manna (bread from heaven) daily. Oh, Jehovah let your ears be attentive to my cry. I worship you and call you holy, holy Lord your holy in your son Jesus name I pray amen.

Bible Verses

"There hath no temptation taken you but such as is common to man: but God is faithful, who will not suffer you to be tempted above that ye are able; but will with the temptation also make a way to escape, that ye may be able to bear it."

- 1 Corinthians 10:13 KJV

"But my God shall supply all your need according to his riches in glory by Christ Jesus." - Philippians 4:19 KJV

"The Lord will perfect that which concerneth me: thy mercy, O Lord, endureth forever: forsake not the works of thine own hands." - Psalm 138: 8 KJV

"Then the Lord said to Moses, "Look, I'm going to rain down food from heaven for you. Each day the people can go out and pick up as much food as they need for that day. I will test them in this to see whether or not they will follow my instructions." - Exodus 16 :4 NLT

"Lord, hear my voice: let thine ears be attentive to the voice of my supplications." - Psalm 130:2 KJV

Prayer 26

God, these bills are piling up I get a call from a bill collector more than I hear from my loved ones. Lord, honestly, if I had the money, I would pay my bills up and off, but I don't have enough income. God, I ask you to enlarge my territory right now, not tomorrow, but now. God cancel out my debt I owe no man anything but to love them. God provide the funds, so this time I will live debt-free. My desires are to tithe, but God, I'm stuck between tithing and keeping the lights on. I know you will come through and provide because God, you are the only source of income I know. You said I am the head and not the tail since I am the head of my household, my children and I are blessed in the city and blessed in the field. I am delighted to know I can talk to you any time, and you answer me in different ways. You speak through me through Bible verses, holy music, people, and my spirit. God don't allow my rent to be late. I can't lose my apartment or my house. I rebuke eviction, repossession, late fees, foreclosure, and low credit score in Jesus' name. Thank you, heavenly father, my children, will never see me, struggling, or live in poverty. I cancel every generational curse and word curse that was attached to me from my bloodline in Jesus' name. Lord, you are the love of my life, and I want you and all of you in Jesus name I pray amen.

Bible Verses

"He was the one who prayed to the God of Israel, "Oh, that

you would bless me and expand my territory! Please be with me in all that I do and keep me from all trouble and pain!" And God granted him his request." - 1 Chronicles 4:10 NLT

"Owe no man anything, but to love one another: for he that loveth another hath fulfilled the law." - Romans 13:8 KJV

"Your towns and your fields will be blessed."
- Deuteronomy 28:3 NLT

"The Lord is nigh unto all them that call upon him, to all that call upon him in truth." - Psalm 145: 18 KJV

"And the Lord shall make thee the head, and not the tail; and thou shalt be above only, and thou shalt not be beneath; if that thou hearken unto the commandments of the Lord thy God, which I command thee this day, to observe and to do them:"
- Deuteronomy 28:13 KJV

Prayer 27

Sweet Jesus oh righteous savior I love worshiping you and blessing your holy name. I am nothing without you I was a lost soul without you but now I found my calling. Lord I will call upon you as long as I live, no one is your equal. Being a mother comes with so much responsibilities. I'm constantly thinking about my baby registry, child's preschool cost, health insurance, and formula. God please provide money for me and my baby's expenses to be completely paid and fully funded by you. Thank you, God, for sending people to give unto my bosom. I will never be broke or cry about financial hardship. Lord I never want to lie for government assistance or harass the father of my child or family members for help because you are my helper. God, I yearn for my child to have the best education on this planet. I ask you to lead me to the right preschool where teachers are anointed to teach and love my child like my child was their very own child. Thank you, God, for not letting this prayer go unanswered in that magnificent name of Jesus I pray amen.

Bible Verses

"Because he hath inclined his ear unto me, therefore will I call upon him as long as I live." - Psalm 116:2 KJV

"Have you never heard? Have you never understood? The Lord is the everlasting God, the Creator of all the earth. He never grows weak or weary. No one can measure the depths of his understanding." - Isaiah 40:28 NLT

69

"Give, and it shall be given unto you; good measure, pressed down, and shaken together, and running over, shall men give into your bosom. For with the same measure that ye mete withal it shall be measured to you again." - Luke 6:38 KJV

"Behold, God is mine helper: The Lord is with them that uphold my soul." - Psalms 54:4 KJV

Prayer 28

Heavenly Father, thank you for waking me up this morning. This morning I direct my prayer to you, and I will look to you. I declare your glory among the nations, your marvelous deeds among all people. I will have no other God but you. Forgive me if all my prayers sound selfish like I'm pleading and begging for signs, miracles, and wonders. God, I want to dedicate this prayer time to just loving on you blessing your holy name. I rather worship you, Lord, who deliver me from the hands of all my enemies. I will always worship you, God, you made the heavens, the earth, the sea, and the springs of water. Lord, anything in me that's not of Christ, I renounce it and ask you to take it away from me. Thank you, God, for washing me white as snow. Lord, I am a single mother at the moment, but I know I seek you, so I will lack no good thing. You're an awesome God, so grateful I have a relationship with you. I love you, God, in that perfect name of your son Jesus I pray amen.

Bible Verses

"My voice shalt thou hear in the morning, O Lord; in the morning will I direct my prayer unto thee and will look up."
- Psalms 5:3 KJV

"Declare his glory among the heathen; his marvelous works among all nations." -1 Chronicles 16:24 KJV

"Thou shalt have no other gods before me." - Exodus 20:3 KJV

"You must worship only the Lord your God. He is the one who will rescue you from all your enemies." - 2 Kings 17:39 NLT

"Fear God," he shouted. "Give glory to him. For the time has come when he will sit as judge. Worship him who made the heavens, the earth, the sea, and all the springs of water." - Revelation 14:7 NLT

"Purify me from my sins, and I will be clean; wash me, and I will be whiter than snow." - Psalms 51:7 NLT

Prayer 29

Lord, as I prepare for bed, I can't stop thinking about how much you love me. You love me more than my mother and father. At times I feel like I'm alone, and no one cares, but God you care because I am supposed to cast my burdens upon you, and you will sustain me. Lord, I don't want to go to the specialist due to pregnancy complications. While I lay down and get my cervix checked, all I can do is plead the blood of Jesus over my body and my baby. I have to be selective to what I agree to when it comes to my pregnancy, all advice isn't Godly advice. God help me to discern the good from the bad in this pregnancy. I have to weed out all of the bad seeds and expose the demons that hide behind the person. God, you are the strength of my heart and my portion forever. God pave the way for me to enjoy this pregnancy, whether I have support or not. I will not compare myself to a woman who seems to have the dream career, husband, and lifestyle. Comparing myself to others only shows how foolish I am, and Lord, I refuse to be foolish. I may be single, but Lord, with you, I can never be lonely. I must stop doubting you, God, and trust you because you know those that trust you. I love you Lord thank you for sending your son to die for my sins in Jesus precious name I pray amen.

Bible Verses

"Cast your burden on the LORD, And He shall sustain you; He shall never permit the righteous to be moved."

- Psalm 55:22 KJV

"My flesh and my heart fail; But God is the strength of my heart and my portion forever." - Psalm 73:26

"Oh, don't worry; we wouldn't dare say that we are as wonderful as these other men who tell you how important they are! But they are only comparing themselves with each other, using themselves as the standard of measurement. How ignorant!" - 2 Corinthians 10:12

"For God so loved the world, that he gave his only begotten Son, that whosoever believeth in him should not perish, but have everlasting life." - John 3:16 KJV

Prayer 30

Lord, this prayer is gender-specific for the baby boy in my womb. I wrote out the vision and made it plain Lord. Before I pray, let me give you honor, praise, and glory because you are worthy to be praised. God, you have saved me from all my enemies. As I come boldly to the throne of God with my petition that I know you will grant if it's your will. God let my son be a worshipper and sing the song of thanks to you, Lord. I ask that my son is rich, like Abraham, with an abundance of everything. Lord, let my son be a perfect and upright man who fears you and turns away from evil like Job. My son will be obedient and do exactly what you command him to do, just like Noah at the beginning of time. This blessing in my womb will please you the same way Enoch pleased you. He will also have wisdom and an understanding heart like Solomon. My baby boy will have meekness, long-suffering, and forbearing one another in love. My son will not die from premature death; he will live a long life and have longevity like Methuselah. God, I want my son to have the Godly traits these men of God had in the Bible. I'm not expecting my son to be these men, but I'm expecting him to have Godly traits that followed these Godly men such as worshipper, wealthy, righteous, faithful, obedient, humble, patience, and longevity. Thank you, Lord, for always answering my prayers in your own way in Jesus name I pray.

Bible Verses

"And the LORD answered me, and said, Write the vision, and

make it plain upon tables, that he may run that readeth it."
- Habakkuk 2:2 KJV

"I will call on the Lord, who is worthy to be praised: so, shall I
be saved from mine enemies." - 2 Samuel 22:4 KJV

"So, let us come boldly to the throne of our gracious God.
There we will receive his mercy, and we will find grace to help
us when we need it most." - Hebrews 4:16 NLT

"Then on that day David delivered first this psalm to thank
the Lord into the hand of Asaph and his brethren."
- 1 Chronicles 16:7 KJV

"And Abram was very rich in cattle, in silver, and in gold."
- Genesis 13:2 KJV

"And the LORD said unto Satan, Hast thou considered my
servant Job, that there is none like him in the earth, a perfect
and an upright man, one that feareth God, and escheweth
evil?" - Job 1:8 KJV

"So, Noah did everything exactly as God had commanded
him." - Genesis 6:22 NLT

"It was by faith that Enoch was taken up to heaven without
dying— "he disappeared, because God took him." For before
he was taken up, he was known as a person who pleased God."
- Hebrews 11:15 NLT

"Behold, I have done according to thy words: lo, I have given
thee a wise and an understanding heart; so that there was none
like thee before thee, neither after thee shall any arise like unto
thee." - 1 King 3:12

"With all lowliness and meekness, with longsuffering, forbearing one another in love;" - Ephesians 4:2 KJV

"Methuselah lived 969 years, and then he died." - Genesis 5:27 NLT

Prayer 31

God grant me tongues so that I can pray in the Holy Ghost. Satan can't understand my heavenly language. Lord, it seems and looks like I wasn't ready to carry this baby girl, but God with you by my side, I'm prepared for everything. I will birth a baby girl who will be a child of God that grows into a righteous woman of God. I ask you that my daughter won't suffer from peer pressure, premarital sex, pre-teen pregnancy, abortions, miscarriages, neonatal death, stillbirth, ectopic pregnancy, depression, oppression, desperation or any attack of Satan. God, I ask that my daughter is patient like Sarah as she waited patiently to conceive Isaac. She will have traits of kindness, just like Naomi, who did not leave her mother-in-law's side. Also, obedient like the widow Zarephath as she listened to the prophet Elijah and saw a miracle for her obedience. In this world, a woman needs to be courageous. Lord, let my daughter be courageous like Jael. She will judge the nations and be a prophetess like the woman of God, Deborah. God bless my baby girl; we will have an unbreakable bond. I will teach her the ways of God, so she will never depart from it. I love you and know you are more than capable of answering my prayer, and you will because you are a God who cannot fail. I love you in your son Jesus name I pray.

Bible Verses

"For he that speaketh in an unknown tongue speaketh not unto

men, but unto God: for no man understandeth him; howbeit in the spirit he speaketh mysteries." - 1 Corinthians 14:2 KJV

"For Sarah conceived, and bare Abraham a son in his old age, at the set time of which God had spoken to him."
- Genesis 21:2 KJV

"And Ruth said, Intreat me not to leave thee, or to return from following after thee: for whither thou goest, I will go; and where thou lodgest, I will lodge: thy people shall be my people, and thy God my God:" - Ruth 1:16

"And she went and did according to the saying of Elijah: and she, and he, and her house, did eat many days." - 1 Kings 17:15 KJV

"But when Sisera fell asleep from exhaustion, Jael quietly crept up to him with a hammer and tent peg in her hand. Then she drove the tent peg through his temple and into the ground, and so he died." - Judges 4:21 NLT

"And Deborah, a prophetess, the wife of Lapidoth, she judged Israel at that time." - Judges 4:4 KJV

"Train up a child in the way he should go and when he is old, he will not depart from it." - Proverbs 22:6 KJV

Prayer 32

Lord, I will praise your name forever and ever, for you have all wisdom and power. I bless your holy name you are the King of Kings and Lord of Lords; you are my everything I give myself to you. God, I want to raise a child that's pleasing in your eyesight and who is not of this world. I would be lying if I say I am perfect and do not make mistakes, but Lord help me to make wise choices when it comes to parenting. I am not raising a hell-raiser; instead, I'm raising a God chaser. No matter how hard it seems, I will discipline my child, which is better than having an undisciplined child who will disgrace me. You have given me this child, and I will read your word to raise my child. Society has multiple ways of parenting as a single mother, but God, your way is the best way ever presented. This child I'm carrying will not forsake your Godly teaching but listen and obey. I will seek your kingdom first, Father God, and everything will be added to me. When I say everything, I mean everything literally. Thank you for being God in Jesus name I pray amen.

Bible Verses

"He said, "Praise the name of God forever and ever, for he has all wisdom and power." - Daniel 2:20 NLT

"Which in his times he shall shew, who is the blessed and only Potentate, the King of kings, and Lord of lords;" - 1 Timothy 6:15 KJV

"And be not conformed to this world: but be ye transformed by the renewing of your mind, that ye may prove what is that good, and acceptable, and perfect, will of God."
- Romans 12:2 KJV

"To discipline a child produces wisdom, but a mother is disgraced by an undisciplined child." - Proverbs 29:15 NLT

"My child listen when your father corrects you. Don't neglect your mother's instruction." - Proverbs 1:8 NLT

"Seek the Kingdom of God above all else, and live righteously, and he will give you everything you need." - Matthew 6:33 NLT

Prayer 33

God, I know I am a spirit living in a fleshly body, but God give me patience to deal with my child. I don't want to snap an end up on the news. I don't want to be the mother who couldn't control her temper and lose a child due to my frustration. I'm called by you to be just, holy, and temperate, so I must have self-control. I am reminded when raising a child alone, it gets complicated I ought to pray without ceasing. God, I ask you for an increase in my strength for the joy of you Lord is my strength. When I feel like cursing, snapping, or fighting stop me in my tracks, don't allow me to act like an untamable wild animal. I didn't plan on being a single mother, but God, you are the father of the fatherless. I ask you to continue to be a good good Father to my child. For your glory, in honor of your purposes, I pray in Jesus' name, amen.

Bible Verses

"But a lover of hospitality, a lover of good men, sober, just, holy, temperate;" - Titus 1:8 KJV

"Pray without ceasing." - 1 Thessalonians 5:17 KJV

"Then he said unto them, go your way, eat the fat, and drink the sweet, and send portions unto them for whom nothing is prepared: for this day is holy unto our Lord: neither be ye sorry; for the joy of the Lord is your strength."
- Nehemiah 8:10 KJV

Single Mother

"A father of the fatherless, and a judge of the widows, is God in his holy habitation." - *Psalms 68:5 KJV*

Prayer 34

God, I come to you with anger in my heart and tears in my eyes. I am frustrated with the grandparents who post my child on social media but wouldn't lift a hand to help me. I am not fake or a phony, so being disrespected by the father of my child's parents is unnecessary stress. Lord I don't care to answer the face time, or any form of video message. How can you call a child once every blue moon and say you love them, but you don't even check on them? Birthdays, Christmas, back to school has passed by but no call or text from grandparents, God not even aunties or uncles. I want to hate the father of my children and his family but that's not your will. I am not supposed to let the sun go down and still be angry. In my anger Lord help me not to sin. I don't want to gossip about the family members of my child or treat them poorly. God give me the desires to be quick to listen, slow to speak and slow to become angry. Teach me how to love my enemies the same way I love myself. God I will be more like you and have mercy with everyone. As I pray you remove these ill feelings, I have towards people open the door for me to be at peace with my enemies in Jesus holy name, I pray amen.

Bible Verses

"Be ye angry, and sin not: let not the sun go down upon your wrath." - Ephesians 4:26 KJV

"Understand this, my dear brothers and sisters: You must all be quick to listen, slow to speak, and slow to get angry."

- James 1:19 NLT

"But I say, love your enemies! Pray for those who persecute you!" - Matthew 5:44 NLT

Prayer 35

God, thank you for protecting me and giving your angels charge over my family and me. It is times where I may not have a babysitter or extra hands, but Lord, thank you for providing the help. My child will not be a victim of molestation, rape, bullying, or any form of violence. Anyone who watches my child while I'm not able to Lord, will care for my child the same way I care for my child. Let my child's caregivers prove to be gentle among you as a nursing mother tenderly cares for her own children. My child will never be afraid to speak up. He/she will use great boldness in their speech. I will never worry about if my child is being mistreated because God, I know you are protecting my child. No one will manipulate my child or brainwash my child. At a very young age, my child will know the difference between right and wrong. My child will not keep a bad company of friends because bad company ruins good morals. God, my child, will do what's right no matter what challenges come their way. I love you Lord, thank you for listening in Jesus name I pray amen.

Bible Verses

"For he shall give his angels charge over thee, to keep thee in all thy ways." - Psalm 91:11 KJV

"But we were gentle among you, even as a nurse cherisheth her children:" - 1 Thessalonians 2:7 KJV

"Seeing then that we have such hope, we use great plainness of

speech:" - 2 Corinthians 3:12 KJV

"The LORD keeps you from all harm and watches over your life." - Psalm 121:7 NLT

"Be not deceived: evil communications corrupt good manners." - 1 Corinthians 15:33 KJV

Prayer 36

God, it's your daughter just dropping by to have some quiet time with you. You are a great King over all the earth. I had my share of men, but God hear me out if there is a man you have ordained me to be with send him my way. Father God forgive me for the times I stepped out of your will and did things my way. Please give me the opportunity again, so I will do things your way this time. I desire to be loved, cherished, and pampered. If it is your will that I marry Lord, bless me with a husband who is fully equipped spiritually and naturally. My husband will live a lifestyle of fasting, praying, tithing, giving, seeking your face, and doing your will. Together we will put on the full armor of God so that we can stand against the wiles of Satan. I made poor choices with men in the past, but Lord grant me wisdom so I can discern if the man is of God or Satan appearing to me as an angel of light. God, I am asking for a husband, but Lord, he will not be a distraction and stop me from fulfilling your will for me. I love you, Lord, and know that if you have a husband for me, he will find me in the right timing in Jesus sinless name I pray amen.

Bible Verses

"For the Lord most high is terrible; he is a great King over all the earth." - Psalm 47:2 KJV

"Put on the whole armour of God, that ye may be able to stand against the wiles of the devil." - Ephesians 6:11 KJV

"If you need wisdom, ask our generous God, and he will give it to you. He will not rebuke you for asking." - James 1:5 NLT

"And no marvel; for Satan himself is transformed into an angel of light." - 2 Corinthians 11:14 KJV

Prayer 37

God, I'm tired of sitting around and being a punching bag to this man. I'm pregnant, and the violence continues. Forgive me for thinking a baby would change his evil ways towards me. God, you were able to change king Saul's heart, which demonstrates how much of a heart fixer you are. I can't even tell you how I got myself in this mess, but Lord get me out of it, please. This man knocked me right off my feet at the beginning, but now he is beating the living daylights out of me. He deceived me just like the serpent deceived Eve in the garden. The material things no longer matter to me anymore. So, what if he paid my tuition, my bills, or took me on a shopping spree, no man is worth my salvation. Lord, you are my rock, salvation, and fortress, I shall not be shaken. Only you, God, have the power to remove me out of this toxic situation. Lord, in my desperation, I'm running to you, not a friend or lover, but you oh God. Stop this man from physically attacking me. It will hurt me to my heart to lose my child over an abusive relationship. Lord fight for me in my silence, give me the strength to leave this man without any ungodly soul tie. I love you and thank you for being a listening hear when I'm up or down in Jesus name I pray Amen.

Bible Verses

"As Saul turned and started to leave, God gave him a new heart, and all Samuel's signs were fulfilled that day."
- 1 Samuel 10:9 NLT

"Now the serpent was more subtil than any beast of the field which the Lord God had made. And he said unto the woman, Yea, hath God said, Ye shall not eat of every tree of the garden?" - Genesis 3:1 KJV

"Now the serpent was more subtil than any beast of the field which the Lord God had made. And he said unto the woman, Yea, hath God said, Ye shall not eat of every tree of the garden?" - Genesis 3:1 KJV

"The Lord shall fight for you, and ye shall hold your peace." - Exodus 14:14 KJV

Chapter Four

Domestic Violence

Prayer 38

God, I need a burning bush experience I want to hear from you. I know I was wrong for sleeping with a married man, but I never thought what I reaped would be this bad. This man is telling me to get an abortion, but when he was spending the nights at my house, he was whispering in my ears, telling me he loves me. God, did you hear him when he said he was leaving his wife for me? He said that they were separated and going through a divorce. That was a lie, and as I go to bed alone every night, he has his wife to go home to. This man never hit me before, but now he feels the need to shove, push, punch, slap, and kick me. I'm a female, and a man has no rights laying his hands on me. I'm sick and tired of covering up my bruises with makeup. My love ones are asking questions, but I'm lying to save myself the embarrassment. This is so embarrassing Lord I never thought life would be this way for me. As much as I want to hate myself, I can't because love covers a multitude of sins. I have been a liar, fornicator, envious, and an adulterer. God, please forgive me of my sins and give me the strength to leave those sins behind me. God, I was mad with his wife, but she is innocent to this situation. God, please be by her side. I know you're near the broken-hearted. Comfort her as she hears and sees me carrying her husband's child in my stomach. Lord, I will not abort this child, but I will lean on you in this pregnancy, and only you in Jesus name I pray amen.

Bible Verses

"And the angel of the Lord appeared unto him in a flame of fire out of the midst of a bush: and he looked, and, behold, the bush burned with fire, and the bush was not consumed."
- Exodus 3:2 KJV

"Be not deceived; God is not mocked: for whatsoever a man soweth, that shall he also reap." - Galatians 6:7 KJV

"Most important of all, continue to show deep love for each other, for love covers a multitude of sins." - 1 Peter 4:8 NLT

"Now repent of your sins and turn to God, so that your sins may be wiped away." - Acts of the Apostles 3:19 NLT

"The Lord is close to the brokenhearted; he rescues those whose spirits are crushed." - Psalms 34:18 NLT

Prayer 39

Oh, gracious and glorious God take your arms and wrap me in them. Hold my hand and never let me go. I need all the love you can give me right now. I feel worthless and shameful. I ignored all the signs of violence and now here I am begging to be in your presence. I feel like nobody loves me or cares. But the song I used to sing as a child *"yes Jesus loves me, for the Bible tells me so"*, keeps playing in my head. God you do love me, and you loved me before I loved myself. I'm here praying that all the bills are paid on time. I'm working overtime to keep a roof over my head while this man sits here and raises his hands to attack me. Lord sometimes I want to kill this man, but thou shall not kill. I have so much evil thoughts running through my head, but Lord I will overcome evil with good. God, I need to spend more time with you, the less time I spend with you the less I feel near to you. Thank you, God, that my pregnancy, this man, or my job doesn't stop me from seeking your face. I love you Holy and righteous King! You are the greatest man who ever walked on this earth. In Jesus name I pray amen.

Bible Verses

"We love him, because he first loved us." - *1 John 4:19 KJV*

"Thou shalt not kill." - *Exodus 20:13 KJV*

"Be not overcome of evil but overcome evil with good."
- *Romans 12:21 KJV*

Prayer 40

I'm so scared to go to the hospital and tell on this man. What if he goes to jail? What if after I have my child, the system snatches my child from me? God, I know you know it takes two parents to raise a child. I don't want to raise a child all alone, but nor do I want a man beating on me or exposing my child to domestic violence. Lord, you hate violence, which is why I know you want me out of this situation. God, I am still able to wake up every morning and pray to you. God, I'm still standing I should have lost my mind a long time ago, but here I am seeking your face. This is a spiritual battle; it is not the man himself but the demons behind him. I ask you to crush the oppressor who is oppressing my life, Jesus destroy the chains in the spiritual realm. I don't want the chains broken because if something is broken, it can be fixed. I want the chains dismantled and of no more. I'm not too fond of bad mouthing this man and speaking negatively about my situation. It's life and death in my tongue so that's why I will speak life in every bad situation. Father God blessings will come out my mouth instead of cursings. God save the man I fathered a child with. Renew his mind, make him over, purify him, and forgive him of his sins. God bless him with a calling and lifestyle like the Apostles in Acts. I repent for everything I have done that does not line up with you in Jesus powerful name I pray amen.

Bible Verses

"The LORD trieth the righteous: but the wicked and him that
98

loveth violence his soul hateth. " - *Psalm 11:5 KJV*

"*Help him to defend the poor, to rescue the children of the needy, and to crush their oppressors.* " - *Psalm 72:4 NLT*

"*Death and life are in the power of the tongue: and they that love it shall eat the fruit thereof.* " - *Proverbs 18:21 KJV*

"*And so, blessing and cursing come pouring out of the same mouth. Surely, my brothers and sisters, this is not right!* "
- James 3:10 NLT

Prayer 41

There is one father, one Son, one Holy Ghost, which is the Godhead and center of my life. God take control of my life; I give you my heart, soul, and mind. I ask you to have your way with me. So many times, I went left when you were telling me to go right. Father God, I ask you to forgive me for disobeying your word because obedience is better than sacrifice. Lord, let this be the last time I live this abusive lifestyle. I turn away from domestic violence. I'm not putting up with a man who doesn't respect me as a woman. I am more precious than jewels, and all things that are desirous cannot compare to me. Thank you, Lord, for opening my eyes, and now I know my worth. I love you, God, and I will obey you in Jesus name, I pray amen.

Bible Verses

"Jesus said unto him, thou shalt love the Lord thy God with all thy heart, and with all thy soul, and with all thy mind."
- Matthew 22:37 KJV

"And Samuel said, Hath the Lord as great delight in burnt offerings and sacrifices, as in obeying the voice of the Lord? Behold, to obey is better than sacrifice, and to hearken than the fat of rams." - 1 Samuel 15:22 KJV

"She is more precious than rubies: and all the things thou canst desire are not to be compared unto her." - Proverbs 3:15 KJV

Prayer 42

God, people say opposites attract like magnets, but this man is entirely different from me, and all we do is fight and argue. Every time I see this man, I feel like I'm in a boxing ring fighting for my life. I will not fear this man because Lord, you are fighting for me. Lord, you are on my side what can man do to me? Absolutely nothing! This has taught me a valuable lesson to depend on you and to read your word daily. Your word is a lamp to my feet. I feel so much better after I spend time in your presence. Thank you, God, for all the ways you comfort me in this difficult time. Help me to see myself the way you see me. I am so wrapped up in the way you love me; at times, it feels unbelievable. I love you, God, with my whole heart even though it doesn't seem like it. I bless your holy name in Your son Jesus name I pray amen.

Bible Verses

"Ye shall not fear them: for the Lord your God he shall fight for you." - *Deuteronomy 3:22 KJV*

"The Lord is on my side; I will not fear: what can man do unto me?" - *Psalms 118:6 KJV*

"Thy word is a lamp unto my feet, and a light unto my path." - *Psalms 119:105 KJV*

Prayer 43

I haven't been myself lately every time I sit down to talk to you; I feel like I am easily distracted. I put you last on my list of priorities when God, you're supposed to be number one in my life. Lord, I need you to increase in me as I decrease. Forgive me, God, for trying to serve you and mammon at the same time. I don't want to be lukewarm, and you spit me out. I want to mean it when I pray to you. You're not a genie in a bottle; I can't just rub you and get three wishes. You're not magic; you're the creator who I owe my life to. God lead me to the right church to join and the right people to fellowship with. I want to be a part of the body of Christ; it's not your will that I live isolated from the things of God. Domestic violence is a closed chapter in my life from here on out I won't allow or submit to any form of violence. I love you, God, today, and every day after today in Jesus name, I pray amen.

Bible Verses

"He must increase, but I must decrease."- John 3:30 KJV

"No man can serve two masters: for either he will hate the one and love the other; or else he will hold to the one and despise the other. Ye cannot serve God and mammon." - Matthew 6:24 KJV

"But since you are like lukewarm water, neither hot nor cold, I will spit you out of my mouth!" - Revelation 3:16 NLT

Prayer 44

God, the safest place in the whole wide world, is in your perfect will. Forgive me, Lord, for stepping out of your perfect will. I tried this thing called life on my own and look where it got me; I feel out of place like I don't know who I am anymore. I know you created me fearfully and wonderfully made, but I feel like I'm in the sea sinking without a life jacket. Lord, I know this isn't the life you have promised for me, but starting today, God I'm believing you will fulfill your promises to me; this is why I will be blessed. Lately, I have been slacking, God, you know plenty times I'm short with my bills and this man pays the balance. I'm really settling for bill money, and that's not what you want for me. Bills are paid, but my body is physically sore. Lord, thank you I am energetic and a hard worker. No longer do I need a man to help me pay bills, but I just need you. God, stop me from thinking negative and help me to start thinking positive. Life can be so overwhelming at times, but God, I found you to be my strength and shield. This man could have killed me or beat me until I had a miscarriage, but you stepped in and saved me. Thank you, Lord, for being my savior. You are my police, paramedic, doctor, nurse, psychiatrist, and psychologist. God continue to show me you still love me every day. I put all my trust in you in Jesus name, I pray amen.

Bible Verses

"I will praise thee; for I am fearfully and wonderfully made

marvelous are thy works; and that my soul knoweth right well." - Psalms 139:14 KJV

"And they had no child, because that Elisabeth was barren, and they both were now well stricken in years. And blessed is she that believed: for there shall be a performance of those things which were told her from the Lord." - Luke 1:7, 45 KJV

"She is energetic and strong, a hard worker." - Proverbs 31:17 NLT

"The Lord is my strength and shield. I trust him with all my heart. He helps me, and my heart is filled with joy. I burst out in songs of thanksgiving." - Psalms 28:7 NLT

Prayer 45

As a child, I sat and watched the women in my family get beaten by men. Now that I'm in a relationship with an abusive man, I see that a generational curse was passed down to me. Lord, I ask that this generational curse stops with me right now. I will no longer take any hits on my physical body, and my mind will not be physically attacked. I rebuke every generational curse that was passed down to me through my bloodline. God, I'm a new creature in Christ, and old things have passed away. This isn't a battle between flesh and blood, but I'm battling against principalities powers, rulers of the darkness of this world, and spiritual wickedness in high places. Father God, I ask you to keep my child and me from every curse, blood covenant, and attack of Satan. I rebuke Satan and all his powers in the name of Jesus. In the name of Jesus, I plead the blood of Jesus over my child and me, everything and everyone connected to me. I will no longer give a place to the devil in my life. I put on the helmet of salvation, I wear the breastplate of faith, my buckle of truth is buckled around me tightly, my feet are prepared with the gospel of peace, I have the sword of the Spirit in my hand and my shield of faith in my other hand, I'm suited for war and covered in your blood Jehovah Nissi in Jesus name I pray amen.

Bible Verses

"This means that anyone who belongs to Christ has become a

new person. The old life is gone; a new life has begun!"
- 2 Corinthians 5:17 NLT

"For we wrestle not against flesh and blood, but against principalities, against powers, against the rulers of the darkness of this world, against spiritual wickedness in high places." - Ephesians 6:12 KJV

"Neither give place to the devil." - Ephesians 4:27 KJV

"Put on the whole armour of God, that ye may be able to stand against the wiles of the devil. For we wrestle not against flesh and blood, but against principalities, against powers, against the rulers of the darkness of this world, against spiritual wickedness in high places. Wherefore take unto you the whole armour of God, that ye may be able to withstand in the evil day, and having done all, to stand. Stand therefore, having your loins girt about with truth, and having on the breastplate of righteousness; And your feet shod with the preparation of the gospel of peace; Above all, taking the shield of faith, wherewith ye shall be able to quench all the fiery darts of the wicked. And take the helmet of salvation, and the sword of the Spirit, which is the word of God: Praying always with all prayer and supplication in the Spirit, and watching thereunto with all perseverance and supplication for all saints;"
- Ephesians 6:11-18 KJV

Prayer 46

Lately, I've been focusing on what I don't have, but Lord, it's so much I still have. I have transportation to and from my destinations; I'm not missing any meals, I have health insurance, whether it's with my profession or Medicaid for pregnant mothers. I have a roof over my head, and as I'm growing in this pregnancy, I still manage to find clothes and shoes I can still fit. Above all, the material things I'm alive and living. The simple fact that I'm on this earth shows me you're not finished with me. God, you are in the midst of me, I shall not be moved, and you will help me. My human mind can't express how good you are. It is your grace, Lord, why I am who I am. Lord though I fall short, I get back up again because it is you; I put my trust in. I can't live without you; I'm desperate to be where you are. This may sound crazy, but God, you said I'm beautiful and beautiful in every way. I'm attractive, and nothing no one says or thinks about me matters. God continue to be a father to me in your son Jesus name I pray amen.

Bible Verses

"God is in the midst of her; she shall not be moved: God shall help her, and that right early." - Psalms 46:5 KJV

"But by the grace of God I am what I am: and his grace which was bestowed upon me was not in vain; but I laboured more abundantly than they all: yet not I, but the grace of God which was with me." - 1 Corinthians 15:10 KJV

"For a just man falleth seven times, and riseth up again: but the wicked shall fall into mischief." - Proverbs 24:16 KJV

"You are altogether beautiful, my darling, beautiful in every way." - Song of Songs 4:7 NLT

Chapter Five

Verbal Abuse

Prayer 47

Lord, today, I feel distraught from all the negative words I heard since I got pregnant. Lord, I'm tired of hearing how I'm messing up my life, how I can't afford a child, the man who I had my child with doesn't love me. I'm am sick and tired of the gossip and drama people bring me when they open up their mouths. Lord give me righteousness and justice for I have been treated unfairly. Lord, I'm asking you to give me beauty for ashes. Stop people from saying negative words to me that only brings me down. God, I ask you to provide me with the wisdom to abstain from every form of evil. God, I will not walk in a spirit of offense if I am wrong Holy Spirit convict me, please. I pray that the people in my circle and I guard our mouths and tongues so that we guard our souls from trouble in Jesus Holy name I pray amen.

Bible Verses

"The Lord gives righteousness and justice to all who are treated unfairly." - *Psalms 103: 6 NLT*

"To appoint unto them that mourn in Zion, to give unto them beauty for ashes, the oil of joy for mourning, the garment of praise for the spirit of heaviness; that they might be called trees of righteousness, the planting of the LORD, that he might be glorified." - *Isaiah 61:3*

"Abstain from all appearance of evil." - *1 Thessalonians 5:22 KJV*

"Whoso keepeth his mouth and his tongue keepeth his soul from troubles." - Proverbs 21:23 KJV

Prayer 48

Today Lord, I'm laying all my burdens down and leaving them with you. Since I have been pregnant verbal abuse has become my life. God, I may have messed up, but you determine who lives, not man. I'm tired of people judging me when you clearly said do not judge, or you too will be judged. Lord, I ask you to give me strength and bless me with peace. God forgive me for everything thing I committed to that was contrary to the word of God. I'm so grateful you're a forgiving God and always right there whenever I need you. Lord, I don't want to be a hypocrite and verbally abuse people because they have verbally abused me. Thank you, Lord, my conversations are always full, with grace, and I have no malice in my hearts towards others. In Jesus mighty name, I pray amen.

Bible Verses

"Give your burdens to the Lord, and he will take care of you. He will not permit the godly to slip and fall." - Psalms 55:22 NLT

"And the Lord God formed man of the dust of the ground and breathed into his nostrils the breath of life; and man became a living soul." - Genesis 2:7 KJV

"Judge not, that ye be not judged." - Matthew 7:1 KJV

"The Lord will give strength unto his people; the Lord will bless his people with peace." - Psalms 29:11 KJV

"Let your speech be always with grace, seasoned with salt, that ye may know how ye ought to answer every man."
- Colossians 4:6 KJV

Prayer 49

God, I feel like I'm at my lowest point right now. When people have babies out of wedlock, I encourage them and love on them. God, I treat people how I want to be treated, so I'm mindful of what I say to others. God, I ask that only gentle words come out of my mouth when a person is vulnerable and facing hardship. God, before I laid down with the father of my child, you knew I was going to conceive a child because you're all-knowing. Your plans are for me to prosper not to harm me. God take full control of my verbal abuse situation and stop everyone who has spoken negative words into me and my child's life. Thank God they repent and stop being negative. Also, forgive me for the times I made anyone feel less of a person. Bring it back to my memory so I can apologize to those who I hurt and make things right with them. Lord, you are good and worthy to be praised in Jesus's perfect name I pray amen.

Bible Verses

"Do to others whatever you would like them to do to you. This is the essence of all that is taught in the law and the prophets."
- Matthew 7:12 NLT

"Gentle words are a tree of life; a deceitful tongue crushes the spirit." - Proverbs 15:4 NLT

Prayer 50

God, I love my baby and haven't even had my first ultrasound. People can be so mean now of days. The father of my child doesn't want to go to any doctor's appointments with me; he wants me to go to the local clinic to kill my child. Killing is a sin that I will have no participation in. God, my baby, growing in me, has my genes and blood flowing through his/her body. You have loved my baby and me with everlasting love, which is another reason to give you a loud praise. Turn to me and have grace on me, Lord, I feel alone in distress. God, I will go to my appointments with a smile on my face because I'm filled with joy that you allowed me to conceive a child. God, you thought so much of me that you decided to make me a parent. Some women have fertility issues, but God, I don't, which is a blessing. For the woman seeking fertility assistance, heal their womb, and their children will be born whole without any fertility treatments. It will cost these women no money to conceive because their bodies will naturally conceive a child after sex with whom you called them to have children with. They will not fear bad news about conceiving a child without medical assistance; they confidently trust that you will care for them. I tell you I love you often, but Lord, I do, and I want you to know I appreciate you and all that you do for mankind in Jesus Magnificent name I pray amen.

Bible Verses

"Long ago the Lord said to Israel: "I have loved you, my

people, with an everlasting love. With unfailing love, I have drawn you to myself." - Jeremiah 31:3 NLT

"Turn to me and have mercy, for I am alone and in deep distress." - Psalms 25:16 NLT

"They do not fear bad news; they confidently trust the Lord to care for them." - Psalms 112:7 NLT

Prayer 51

I love the way you love me, Lord. I have made poor choices, but God, you're so loving and forgiving I can see tomorrow. God, I feel like it's an accomplishment I'm deciding to mother my biological child instead of throwing my trash in the garbage. I'm willing to be the best mother to this child, but still, I have people around me who are using their words to hurt me. I'm not asking for worldly advice, but that's what they're giving me. I'm told I don't make enough money, apply for government assistance, I'm going to struggle, this the worse decision I made, I'm too smart to have a child out of wedlock or a child with this man. God, these words aren't uplifting or encouraging. You ask us to edify one another, so that's what I'm expecting. God forgive those who offended me with their words knowingly and unknowingly. God, when I'm put in the situation to speak my mind or give advice. Lord, please let me do it with love and not from my flesh in Jesus name, I pray amen.

Bible Verses

"But God, who is rich in mercy, for his great love wherewith he loved us," - Ephesians 2:4 KJV

"In whom we have redemption through his blood, the forgiveness of sins, according to the riches of his grace;" - Ephesians 1:7 KJV

"Wherefore comfort yourselves together, and edify one another, even as also ye do." - 1 Thessalonians 5:11 KJV

"And do everything with love." - *1 Corinthians 16:14 NLT*

Prayer 52

Lord, despite what anyone says about me, I know what you say I am. I am a part of your household Lord. Jesus, you love me and gave yourself to me. You're the reason Lord why I don't walk in condemnation. I am never alone, God, because you are with me. I am fearfully and wonderfully made. You have given me freedom. God, you chose me. I didn't choose you. God, thank you for letting me know I am your beloved daughter in Jesus name I pray.

Bible Verses

"Now therefore ye are no more strangers and foreigners, but fellowcitizens with the saints, and of the household of God;"
- Ephesians 2:19 KJV

"I am crucified with Christ: nevertheless, I live; yet not I, but Christ liveth in me: and the life which I now live in the flesh I live by the faith of the Son of God, who loved me, and gave himself for me." - Galatians 2:20 KJV

"There is therefore now no condemnation to them which are in Christ Jesus, who walk not after the flesh, but after the Spirit."
- Romans 8:1 KJV

"Behold, the hour cometh, yea, is now come, that ye shall be scattered, every man to his own, and shall leave me alone: and yet I am not alone, because the Father is with me."
- John 16:32 KJV

"I will praise thee; for I am fearfully and wonderfully made marvelous are thy works; and that my soul knoweth right well." - Psalms 139:14 KJV

"If the Son therefore shall make you free, ye shall be free indeed." - John 8:36 KJV

"Since God chose you to be the holy people he loves, you must clothe yourselves with tenderhearted mercy, kindness, humility, gentleness, and patience." - Colossians 3:12 NLT

Prayer 53

God, if it was ever a time, I put negative words above what you said about me forgive me, Lord. I ask that I am bold as a lion and stop verbal abuse at the tongue of mouths. God, don't let the stuff people used to attack my character tear me down. Talking too much leads to sin but being quiet leads to wisdom. God, I rebuke every form of verbal abuse in my life; it will not affect my unborn child or me. I came too far to give up on you, God. This pregnancy is my testimony, and you said we overcome by the blood of the lamb and every word of our testimony. God, you allowed me to conceive, so I know you have the power to shut down verbal abuse immediately in my life. Lord, do the impossible with words in my life in your son Jesus name I pray Amen.

Bible Verses

"The wicked run away when no one is chasing them, but the godly are as bold as lions." - Proverbs 28:1 NLT

"Too much talk leads to sin. Be sensible and keep your mouth shut." - Proverbs 10:19 NLT

"And they have defeated him by the blood of the Lamb and by their testimony. And they did not love their lives so much that they were afraid to die." - Revelation 12:11 NLT

"But Jesus beheld them, and said unto them, with men this is impossible; but with God all things are possible."

- Matthew 19:26 KJV

Prayer 54

God, you know all and see all you know my situation. I ask that you give me the strength to make the right decision with the people I let in my life. Lord forgive the people who did me wrong knowingly I won't repay evil with evil. I will give it to you. Lord, you said I'm fearfully and wonderfully made. I am beautiful and beautiful in every way. You decide who gives life, and you blessed me with this child. I ask you to comfort me and show me your face. Lord, I want you to show me who you really are the same God that freed the Israelites in Egypt, the same God who protected Noah and his family from the Flood. The same God who shut the lion's mouth when Daniel was thrown in the lion's den. Jesus, you said you will never leave me or forsake me, please stay by my side and wrap me in your loving arms. You told me I'm the apple of your eyes. God, I rebuke every curse in my life and every generational demon that is present in my life. Forgive me of every sin I committed willingly and unwillingly. Lord, I ask you that from here on out, you expand my territory, and I will have no lack. I will never struggle I declare and decree the blessings of the Lord has made me rich and added no sorrow with it. I love you, Lord, in your holy son Jesus name I pray amen.

Bible Verses

"The eyes of the Lord are in every place, beholding the evil and the good." - Proverbs 15:3 KJV

"Don't repay evil for evil. Don't retaliate with insults when

people insult you. Instead, pay them back with a blessing. That is what God has called you to do, and he will grant you his blessing." - 1 Peter 3:9 NLT

"I will praise thee; for I am fearfully and wonderfully made marvelous are thy works; and that my soul knoweth right well." - Psalms 139:14 KJV

"You are altogether beautiful, my darling, beautiful in every way." - Song of Songs 4:7 NLT

"Be strong and of a good courage, fear not, nor be afraid of them: for the Lord thy God, he it is that doth go with thee; he will not fail thee, nor forsake thee." - Deuteronomy 31:6 KJV

"Keep me as the apple of the eye, hide me under the shadow of thy wings," - Psalms 17:8 KJV

"Even strong young lions sometimes go hungry, but those who trust in the Lord will lack no good thing." - Psalms 34:10 NLT

"The blessing of the Lord makes a person rich, and he adds no sorrow with it." - Proverbs 10:22 NLT

Prayer 55

God, thank you for renewing my mind. I'm going to trust your word and believe whatever I pray if I believe what I pray it will come to pass. You are my hiding place and my shield I know you will keep verbal abuse from me. When I cry to you, God, you answer me. Thank you, God, for listening and answering all my cries. God give me the strength to keep your commandments, knowing that everything thing I ask of you I will receive. God, let me find the exact Bible verse or chapter you want me to read while I take this journey called motherhood. I want to be in your will because being outside your will led me to sin, and the wages of sin is death. I will no longer follow the trends of this world but take up my cross and be a follower of Christ in Jesus name I pray amen.

Bible Verses

"Therefore, I say unto you, what things soever ye desire, when ye pray, believe that ye receive them, and ye shall have them."
- Mark 11:24 KJV

"Thou art my hiding place and my shield: I hope in thy word."
- Psalms 119:114 KJV

"In the day when I cried, thou answeredst me, and strengthenedst me with strength in my soul."
- Psalms 138:3 KJV

"And whatsoever we ask, we receive of him, because we keep

his commandments, and do those things that are pleasing in his sight." - 1 John 3:22 KJV

"For the wages of sin is death; but the gift of God is eternal life through Jesus Christ our Lord." - Romans 6:23 KJV

"Then said Jesus unto his disciples, if any man will come after me, let him deny himself, and take up his cross, and follow me." - Matthew 16:24 KJV

Prayer 56

Lord God, you leave me speechless day after day. I don't deserve to be a mother, but you still did it for me. I lived a promiscuous lifestyle, and I'm pregnant from a verbal abuser, but God, my baby, is safely growing in my womb. I repented for my wild and crazy lifestyle, and you forgave me once I repented. God, I'm grateful my inner man is renewed every day. All my life, I listened to what people told me, but now I'm listening to your words God. The word of God is a weapon against my enemies. God, you blessed me with the opportunity to turn my life around. I could have been dead or in jail, but because of your love for me, I am here pregnant and saying this prayer. Lord verbal abuse is a thing of the past for me. I put on the new man, which is the righteous holy me who is pleasing in your eyesight. God, I adore you and worship you in spirit, and in truth, in Jesus' perfect name, I pray amen.

Bible Verses

"Then he says, 'I will never again remember their sins and lawless deeds.'" - Hebrews 10:17 NLT

"For which cause we faint not; but though our outward man perish, yet the inward man is renewed day by day."
- 2 Corinthians 4:16 KJV

"And that ye put on the new man, which after God is created in righteousness and true holiness." - Ephesians 4:24 KJV

"God is a Spirit: and they that worship him must worship him in spirit and in truth." - John 4:24 KJV

Prayer 57

God use me however you want to use me. Wherever you need me to go and whatever you need me to do I will do. The harvest is plentiful, but the laborers are few, so I ask that you send me. You blessed me with a child, and I know every good gift comes from you father God. Teach me self-love God, you are love therefore teaching me how to love is your specialty. When my enemies use verbal abuse to come up against me like a flood you lift up a standard against my enemies. God I'm acknowledging you in all my ways and you shall direct my path. God stop me from walking down the wrong direction reveal yourself to me and correct my mistakes and lead me to the direction you have set aside for me. God thank you for being so loving and patient with me. I wouldn't be here if it wasn't for you. God you are amazing, and you love me flaws and all. I surrender all to you in Jesus name I pray amen.

Bible Verses

"Then saith he unto his disciples, the harvest truly is plenteous, but the labourers are few;" - Matthew 9:37 KJV

"Every good gift and every perfect gift is from above, and cometh down from the Father of lights, with whom is no variableness, neither shadow of turning." - James 1:17 KJV

"He that loveth not knoweth not God; for God is love." - 1 John 4:8 KJV

"So, shall they fear the name of the Lord from the west, and his glory from the rising of the sun. When the enemy shall come in like a flood, the Spirit of the Lord shall lift up a standard against him." - Isaiah 59:19 KJV

"In all thy ways acknowledge him, and he shall direct thy paths." - Proverbs 3:6 KJV

Chapter Six

Depression

Prayers for the Forgotten Single Expectant Mother

Prayer 58

It's time to bring the big guns out. Satan has been attacking me for too long now; I got the real warriors on my side God, Jesus, and the Holy Ghost. The devil is no match for you; God; he was thrown out of heaven and lost his position. Through you Lord, I will push down my enemies, through your holy name, I will tread over those who rise against me. I am no longer afraid or discouraged because this battle isn't mines; it's the Lord. God, you are for me nothing can come against me. I wasn't born depressed, and I won't live depressed. Whatever I need supply for me, Lord, for you are the only need supplier I know. Get thee behind me Satan you have no authority over me because I'm a child of God. There is no sin you can hold over my head devil because I repented, and God is so gracious he forgave and forgot my sins. Thank you, Lord, for securing me in your hands in Jesus matchless name I pray amen.

Bible Verses

"And there was war in heaven: Michael and his angels fought against the dragon; and the dragon fought and his angels and prevailed not; neither was their place found any more in heaven." - Revelation 12:7-8 KJV

"Through thee will we push down our enemies: through thy name will we tread them under that rise up against us." - Psalms 44:5 KJV

"But my God shall supply all your need according to his

riches in glory by Christ Jesus." - Philippians 4:19 KJV

"But he turned, and said unto Peter, get thee behind me, Satan: thou art an offence unto me: for thou savourest not the things that be of God, but those that be of men." - Matthew 16:23 KJV

"And I will forgive their wickedness, and I will never again remember their sins." - Hebrews 8:12 NLT

"for my Father has given them to me, and he is more powerful than anyone else. No one can snatch them from the Father's hand." - John 10:29 NLT

Prayer 59

Lift up my soul, oh Lord right now I feel so low like I will never get back up. I hate my situation; the more I think of it, the lower I feel. I don't want to pray, pick up the phone, or even spend time with you. It's that bad God I feel like my life is heading down a path of destruction. I know it is not your will for me to be depressed or oppressed you came so that I can have life and have it more abundantly. The same way Jesus overcame the world, I ask you that I overcome my situation. Satan is the author of confusion and the joy snatcher. I plead the blood of Jesus over my health right now, father God. I am whole in the name of Jesus. I am not depressed or need anti-depressants. The only counselor I need is the wonderful counselor Jesus. God, it is no shortage of blessings in your storehouse. I trust and believe that I have my peace and joy back. As a matter of fact, Lord, I got my life back. Satan, you have no power in my life, future, and unborn child I rebuke every dart you are throwing at me. Every single dart you have thrown has been returned to sender and will never reach its original target in Jesus mighty and robust name I pray amen.

Bible Verses

"Cause me to hear thy lovingkindness in the morning; for in thee do I trust cause me to know the way wherein I should walk; for I lift up my soul unto thee." - Psalms 143:8 KJV

"The thief cometh not, but for to steal, and to kill, and to destroy I am come that they might have life, and that they might

have it more abundantly." - John 10:10 KJV

"These things I have spoken unto you, that in me ye might have peace. In the world ye shall have tribulation: but be of good cheer; I have overcome the world." - John 16:33 KJV

"For unto us a child is born, unto us a son is given, and the government shall be upon his shoulder: and his name shall be called Wonderful, Counsellor, The mighty God, The everlasting Father, The Prince of Peace." - Isaiah 9:6 KJV

"The Lord shall open unto thee his good treasure, the heaven to give the rain unto thy land in his season, and to bless all the work of thine hand: and thou shalt lend unto many nations, and thou shalt not borrow." - Deuteronomy 28:12 KJV

Prayer 60

Beautiful father, you are more beautiful than the flowers that grow on trees. Your love is unstoppable and unforgettable. Medical physicians and loved ones are telling me I'm depressed, and depression has the worse effect on babies. God, I'm not accepting depression! No, I'm not depressed; I'm happy and excited about my new life with my child. I decided to come to you instead of running to people with my business. Grant me favor for a lifetime. As I walk through the valley of depression, I will fear no evil, you are with me, and you comfort me. Every test I take the results will come back perfect; I will never be required to have extra testing done. Everything is worked out for my good because I love you, and I'm called according to your purpose. Thank you for being God and the one and only God in Jesus name I pray amen.

Bible Verses

"Come unto me, all ye that labour and are heavy laden, and I will give you rest." - Matthew 11:28 KJV

"For his anger endureth but a moment; in his favour is life: weeping may endure for a night but joy cometh in the morning." - Psalms 30:5 KJV

"Yea, though I walk through the valley of the shadow of death, I will fear no evil: for thou art with me; thy rod and thy staff they comfort me." - Psalms 23:4 KJV

"And we know that all things work together for good to them that love God, to them who are the called according to his purpose." - *Romans 8:28 KJV*

Prayer 61

God, I'm sitting here working on this job 8 hours a day. My coworkers keep up gossip, my supervisors treat me poorly, and I'm underpaid. I understand if I don't work, I won't eat; that's why I'm on time for my job every day. God, it's depressing to think about working at a job where my work is unappreciated, but God, this is just a season in my life. Use me, God, that you will be perfected in my work at my job. Lord my situation will change before my child comes because I abide in your word and your word abides in me what I ask will be done unto me in Jesus name I pray amen.

Bible Verses

*"Even while we were with you, we gave you this command: "Those unwilling to work will not get to eat." -
2 Thessalonians 3:10 NLT*

"To everything there is a season, and a time to every purpose under the heaven:" - Ecclesiastes 3:1 KJV

"That the man of God may be perfect, thoroughly furnished unto all good works." - 2 Timothy 3:17 KJV

"If ye abide in me, and my words abide in you, ye shall ask what ye will, and it shall be done unto you." - John 15:7 KJV

Prayer 62

God, it's your good pleasure to give me the kingdom. Nowhere in your word, I read that you want me to be abused and misused. God, I'm not sure what is the exact cause of this spirit of depression, but I will continue to do your will and receive all that you have promised me. It's so much power in my tongue Lord I will speak your word versus what my flesh wants me to speak. Your word I hide in my heart so that I don't sin against you. Thank you, God, for increasing my strength every time I feel powerless. I rebuke the hands of Satan over my life and my unborn child's life. Lord, you are faithful; you established me and continue to keep me from the evil one. Thank you, God, for always having my front, back, left, and right in Jesus' magnificent name, I pray amen.

Bible Verses

"Fear not, little flock; for it is your Father's good pleasure to give you the kingdom." - Luke 12:32 KJV

"Patient endurance is what you need now, so that you will continue to do God's will. Then you will receive all that he has promised." - Proverbs 18:21 KJV

"Death and life are in the power of the tongue: and they that love it shall eat the fruit thereof." - Hebrews 10:36 NLT

"I have hidden your word in my heart, that I might not sin against you." - Psalm 119:11

"He giveth power to the faint; and to them that have no might he increaseth strength." - *Isiah 40:29 KJV*

"But the Lord is faithful, who shall stablish you, and keep you from evil." - *2 Thessalonians 3:3 KJV*

Prayer 63

For the weapons of my warfare are not carnal but mighty through God to the pulling down of strongholds. This battle of fighting isn't with my natural eyes; it's completely spiritual. Lord, you have armed me with strength for the battle; you have subdued my enemies under my feet. Thank you, Jesus; my enemies are under my feet! I am submitting myself to you, God, resisting the devil, and Satan has no choice but to flee immediately! I cancel out every single demonic spirit that is associated with depression in my life right now in Jesus' name. My child in my womb, my living children, and children to come are free from the spirit of depression right now in Jesus' name. God, I ask you to move swiftly on my behalf and deliver me from every spirit in my life that is not the Holy Spirit. I will be holy for you are holy father, God. Lord, I want to be a faithful servant to you for the rest of my life. Remove boundaries and obstacles that stop me from being your daughter. I love you, God, and appreciate you being the best father a girl can have. Thank you, God, for loving me even when I mess up in Jesus name, I pray amen.

Bible Verses

"For the weapons of our warfare are not carnal, but mighty through God to the pulling down of strong holds"
- 2 Corinthians 10:4 KJV

"You have armed me with strength for the battle; you have subdued my enemies under my feet." - 2 Samuel 22:40 NLT

144

"Submit yourselves therefore to God. Resist the devil, and he will flee from you." - James 4:7 KJV

Prayer 64

God, this isn't my first time having a child. I have a toddler at home and a baby on the way. The father of my child splits daycare and buys the latest and the greatest for our child. I appreciate his financial help and can't complain, but I need physical help that's permanent. With one child, I wanted to throw in the towel now I have another one in my womb. I'm not accepting depression or saying I'm depressed. I'm the opposite of depressed: cheerful, glad, happy, joyful, and peaceful. Thank you, Lord, for comforting me the same way a mother comforts her child. Holy Spirit bless me with the nine gifts of your spirit (love, joy, peace, long-suffering, gentleness, goodness, faith, meekness, and temperance). The duties that come with being a mother will not burden me but improve my mothering skills in Jesus name I pray amen.

Bible Verses

"I will comfort you there in Jerusalem as a mother comforts her child." - Isaiah 66:13 NLT

"But the fruit of the Spirit is love, joy, peace, longsuffering, gentleness, goodness, faith, Meekness, temperance: against such there is no law." - Galatians 5:22-23 KJV

Prayer 65

God carrying another child comes with more expenses. I have to eat more food, buy more clothes, shoes, pay copayments at my doctor's office, and purchase items for my unborn child. Lord I'm already living paycheck to paycheck sometimes my checks are short. My credit is low and I can't even get a credit card or payday loan. Whether I conceived this child through marriage or fornication, I decided to carry my child regardless of abortion clinics being available. God forgive me for every sin I committed before this pregnancy and during this pregnancy. Lord you are just and faithful to forgive me of all my sins and purify me from unrighteousness. The cares of the world will not leave me depressed because one thing you don't do is lie. You promised me life and life more abundantly not depression. Thank you, God, for being available to me anytime in your son Jesus holy name I pray amen.

Bible Verses

"If we confess our sins, he is faithful and just to forgive us our sins, and to cleanse us from all unrighteousness." - 1 John 1:9 KJV

"By his divine power, God has given us everything we need for living a godly life. We have received all of this by coming to know him, the one who called us to himself by means of his marvelous glory and excellence." - 2 Peter 1:3 NLT

"God is not a man, that he should lie; neither the son of man,

that he should repent: hath he said, and shall he not do it? or hath he spoken, and shall he not make it good?"
- Numbers 23:19 KJV

"The thief cometh not, but for to steal, and to kill, and to destroy: I am come that they might have life, and that they might have it more abundantly." - John 10:10 KJV

Prayer 66

Precious Jesus, I'm so glad that you rose on the third day and showed me how to live my life here on this earth. The Holy Spirit was able to come upon me and give me power. I was granted the power to heal sickness and cast out devils. Satan today, I'm serving you and your whole hierarchy! I'm serving you all notice today with the blood of Jesus. I rebuke the spirit of sorrow, confusion, rejection, sadness, suicide, depression, discouragement, defeat, frustration, curses, and apathy in the name of Jesus. The spirit of failure has to bow down right now by the blood of Jesus. I'm done battling with demons, today Lord, I put you above my situation and lay it all down at your feet. My baby and I are covered under your blood, sweet Jesus. Nothing will ever stop your love from flowing to me, father God. I can't help but love you more and more every day. It feels like a dream, Jesus, how generous you are to me. Thank you Lord I remain in your will in Jesus name I pray amen.

Bible Verses

"And he said, "Yes, it was written long ago that the Messiah would suffer and die and rise from the dead on the third day."
- Luke 24:46 NLT

"But ye shall receive power, after that the Holy Ghost is come upon you: and ye shall be witnesses unto me both in Jerusalem, and in all Judaea, and in Samaria, and unto the uttermost part of the earth." - Acts 1:8 KJV

"And to have power to heal sicknesses, and to cast out devils:"
- Mark 3:15 KJV

Prayer 67

Lord, I won't be afraid I will believe everything you promised me and my seed. God, I know you have put my enemies to shame as you help and comfort me. I wasn't born depressed, and I'm not claiming to be depressed. God, you are too good for me to sit around and let my adversary use my mind as his playing field. Lord, let your unfailing love comfort me just as you promised. Satan can't steal the promises you have set aside for my child and me. God, thank you for taking me higher even when I feel like I hit rock bottom. In my sin, you still loved me. Lord, you don't cast your people off forever; you're so accepting. Thank you for accepting my child and me in Jesus name I pray amen.

Bible Verses

"As soon as Jesus heard the word that was spoken, he saith unto the ruler of the synagogue, Be not afraid, only believe."
- Mark 5:36 KJV

"Send me a sign of your favor. Then those who hate me will be put to shame, for you, O Lord, help and comfort me."
- Psalms 86:17 NLT

"Now let your unfailing love comfort me, just as you promised me, your servant." - Psalms 119:76 NLT

"For the Lord will not cast off for ever:" - Lamentations 3:31 KJV

Prayer 68

Lord, my adversary, is out to get me! God, you brought me in this predicament so I could save many lives. Lord this is my testimony you are allowing this to happen so I can witness and uplift others who came face to face with the spirit of depression. Thank you, Lord, I overcame by the blood of the lamb and every word of my testimony. In the midst of this situation, I still feel your love, father, God. Continue to rejoice over me with joy, father, God. I will not doubt you, Lord, because wavered faith is like a wave of the sea driven with the wind and tossed. It doesn't matter how many times Satan wants me to question your power because I know your real, and your word comes alive in me every single time I read it. Lord, I'm looking unto you, and you will hear me. Before my child is born, I am depression free and will not suffer from postpartum depression. In Jesus' righteous name, I pray amen.

Bible Verses

"You intended to harm me, but God intended it all for good. He brought me to this position so I could save the lives of many people." - Genesis 50:20 NLT

"And they overcame him by the blood of the Lamb, and by the word of their testimony; and they loved not their lives unto the death." - Revelation 12:11 KJV

"The Lord thy God in the midst of thee is mighty; he will save, he will rejoice over thee with joy; he will rest in his love, he

will joy over thee with singing." - Zephaniah 3:17 KJV

"But let him ask in faith, nothing wavering. For he that wavereth is like a wave of the sea driven with the wind and tossed." - James 1:6 KJV

"Therefore, I will look unto the Lord; I will wait for the God of my salvation: my God will hear me." - Micah 7:7 KJV

Prayer 69

I will rejoice in my current state, knowing problems and trials help me develop endurance. Before this incident, I was slacking with my relationship with you. I prayed less, barely read the Bible, didn't fast, wouldn't tithe, and went to church only when I was in the mood. Forgive me, God, for treating you like an elective in school that is not necessary for my diploma. Jesus, I want to know your glory and your power. I will trust in you at all times, pour out my heart before you. It feels good knowing I have you in my corner and that you God are fighting my battle for me. I walked into this situation weak as a cub; now, I'm standing bold and strong as a lion. God depression is no match for your mighty power. Jesus, you walked on water, you raised the dead, you cast out devils. You did all this just to show me no evil spirit can live in me once you get a hold of my heart, mind, body, and soul. You are the father I never had, the savior who keeps saving, and the provider who always provides. Loving you was the best decision I made in this pregnancy. I love you, gracious father in Jesus' perfect name I pray amen.

Bible Verses

"We can rejoice, too, when we run into problems and trials, for we know that they help us develop endurance." - Romans 5:3 NLT

"Trust in him at all times; ye people, pour out your heart before him: God is a refuge for us. Selah." - Psalms 62:8 KJV

"The Lord your God which goeth before you, he shall fight for you, according to all that he did for you in Egypt before your eyes;" - Deuteronomy 1:30 KJV

"And in the fourth watch of the night Jesus went unto them, walking on the sea." - Matthew 14:25 KJV

"And besought him greatly, saying, My little daughter lieth at the point of death: I pray thee, come and lay thy hands on her, that she may be healed; and she shall live." - Mark 5:23 KJV

"And he took the damsel by the hand, and said unto her, Talitha cumi; which is, being interpreted, Damsel, I say unto thee, arise. And straightway the damsel arose, and walked; for she was of the age of twelve years. And they were astonished with a great astonishment." - Mark 5:41-42 KJV

Chapter Seven

Teenage Pregnancy

Prayer 70

Heavenly Father, I'm a minor and pregnant. All I can think about is how I let my family down. I'm ashamed to go to school, church, or family events. I sense that when I walk in the room, everyone is staring or talking about me. I'm too young to be pregnant, but I had sexual intercourse, and pregnancy is a result of sex. Lord give me the strength to have this baby and be the number one mother in the region. God, my child, is a gift from you and a reward from you. Thank you, God, my baby, is heaven-sent. I will wait on you, Lord, as you renew my strength. I will fear not cause Lord you will help me raise my child. I will graduate from high school on time. My child will live a blessed life, and what I went through my child would never go through. Thank you, God, for listening to my prayers and forgiving me of my sins in Jesus name I pray amen.

Bible Verses

"Children are a gift from the Lord; they are a reward from him." - Psalms 127:3 NLT

"But they that wait upon the Lord shall renew their strength; they shall mount up with wings as eagles; they shall run, and not be weary; and they shall walk, and not faint."
- Isaiah 40:31 KJV

"For I the Lord thy God will hold thy right hand, saying unto thee, Fear not; I will help thee." - Isaiah 41:13 KJV

"For I will be merciful to their unrighteousness, and their sins and their iniquities will I remember no more." - *Hebrews 8:12 KJV*

Prayer 71

God, the father of my child, is upset I'm pregnant, but he wasn't upset when he helped me conceive our child. I always thought I would be married, and all my kids come from my husband, but look, this man isn't even interested in having a baby with me. I feel bamboozled and like a fool. I was giving my all to someone who wasn't even giving me ten percent. I want to curse, act a fool, and slander the father of my child. Help me, Lord, to stop my anger and allow my words to be pleasing to you. I will not retaliate or seek to destroy the father of my child; Lord vengeance belongs to you. Just as Christ forgave me, I will forgive the father of my child. God, you know if this man will stick around and help, but if he doesn't thank you, Jesus, for supplying me and my child's every need in Jesus' magnificent name, I pray amen.

Bible Verses

"May the words of my mouth and the meditation of my heart be pleasing to you, O Lord, my rock and my redeemer."
- Psalms 19:14 NLT

"Dearly beloved, avenge not yourselves, but rather give place unto wrath: for it is written, Vengeance is mine; I will repay, saith the Lord." - Romans 12:19 KJV

"And be ye kind one to another, tenderhearted, forgiving one another, even as God for Christ's sake hath forgiven you."

- Ephesians 4:32 KJV

"But my God shall supply all your need according to his riches in glory by Christ Jesus." - Philippians 4:19 KJV

Prayer 72

How can I be pregnant? I have no parents, and my living condition is below the poverty level. Sometimes I have to pray and wait for my next meal to come. If it weren't for free meals at school, I wouldn't eat breakfast or lunch Monday - Friday. I heard in sex education use condoms or practice abstinence; God I didn't do any of the above. I'm not even in a relationship with the guy who knocked me up. He is young and immature; it's a possibility I'm pregnant, and someone else is carrying his child as well. The only thing stopping me from giving up on life is this baby inside me. Lord let heaven's armies be here among my child and me, you are my fortress. Forgive me of my sins, God all humans fall short of the glory of God, but I am made right in your sight because of Jesus Christ. God, if the father wants to help, thank you, Jesus, I'm not bitter, and I allow him to help. Father God, I ask you to stop anyone from gossiping about me and spreading rumors because slandering others makes you a fool. Send the right people to counsel me so that I make wise decisions. When I walk, I won't be held back, when I run, I won't stumble because God you love me more than I ever love myself. Thank you, God, for being the lover of my soul in Jesus name I pray amen.

Bible Verses

"The Lord of Heaven's Armies is here among us; the God of Israel is our fortress. Interlude" - Psalms 46:7 NLT

"For all have sinned, and come short of the glory of God; Being justified freely by his grace through the redemption that is in Christ Jesus:" - Romans 3:23-24 KJV

"Hiding hatred makes you a liar; slandering others makes you a fool." - Proverbs 10: 18 NLT

"Without counsel purposes are disappointed: but in the multitude of counsellors they are established." - Proverbs 15:22 KJV

"When you walk, you won't be held back; when you run, you won't stumble." - Proverbs 4:12 NLT

Prayer 73

Jesus, I come to you with a heart full of sorrow and an eye filled with tears. I found myself seeing a man who is old enough to be my uncle. This man has wined and dined me, he told me I was beautiful, he bought me a phone, new shoes, the list goes on. I don't come from a household where eating out is typical, or bills are paid on time. My parents couldn't afford to do the things this man was doing for me. Kids get bullied when they wear hand me downs, faded clothes, non-name brand shoes. It was bad enough; my hair was never done. After meeting this man, he turned my world upside down. I felt like I went from rags to riches. How could something so perfect fall into pieces right before my eyes. It's against the law for him to have sexual relations with me. He wasn't looking for a wife; he was looking for a thrill. God forgive me for being naive and following the trends of this world. God, don't let your kindness depart from me, or your covenant of peace be removed from me. Please continue to have mercy on my soul. I love you because you heard my voice and my supplication. I'm scared to tell my parents due to my age and our financial status but thank you, Lord, my parents, don't kick me out or abandon me. God allow my health insurance to cover my pregnancy and my baby. I will have no pregnancy complications or illnesses. God, you know if this man is full of STDS, I ask you Lord that you shield my baby and me from every sexually transmitted disease a human body can carry. I plead the blood of Jesus over my unborn child, my family, me, and the father of my child.

I bind up every single attack of the enemy with the blood of Jesus. God don't reject my child or me. Give me the mindset to care for my child. I will not be unfit or neglect my child. My child and I will see the Lord's goodness while we are here in the land of the living. Thank you for being my refuge and safe place when I'm in distress in Jesus powerful name I pray amen.

Bible Verses

"For the mountains shall depart, and the hills be removed; but my kindness shall not depart from thee, neither shall the covenant of my peace be removed, saith the Lord that hath mercy on thee." - Isaiah 54:10 KJV

"I love the Lord, because he hath heard my voice and my supplications." - Psalms 116:1 KJV

"Yet I am confident I will see the Lord's goodness while I am here in the land of the living." - Psalms 27:13 NLT

"But as for me, I will sing about your power. Each morning I will sing with joy about your unfailing love. For you have been my refuge, a place of safety when I am in distress." - Psalms 59:16 NLT

Prayer 74

I'm big and pregnant, and he can fix his mouth to tell me to get tested. How can I be so stupid to give all of me to a man who to him I'm just another girl with a vagina between my legs. He whispered sweet nothings in my ear, broke all his promises, lied time after time, but I always take him back. God, I have so much rage in me! I can go over there right now and bust him and his mama windows all out, break his game system, and tv. I would bleach all his clothes and shoes then set them on fire, but your word said, don't let evil conquer me but conquer evil by doing good. I will obey your word and just lay it down on you, Jesus. I know I wouldn't want anyone to treat me the way he treated me. I treat people the way I want to be treated. As you instruct me to do, I will bless them that curse me and pray for them who intentionally use me. Forgive me, God, for being a child pregnant with a child. Forgive me for disobeying you when I fornicated and lived a lifestyle of fornication. Now times of refreshing are available to me, for I have repented and decided not to sin anymore. I love you, Father God, in Jesus matchless name I pray amen.

Bible Verses

"Don't let evil conquer you, but conquer evil by doing good."
- Romans 12:21 NLT

"Do to others as you would like them to do to you."
- Luke 6:31 NLT

"Bless them that curse you, and pray for them which despitefully use you." - Luke 6:28 KJV

"Repent ye therefore, and be converted, that your sins may be blotted out, when the times of refreshing shall come from the presence of the Lord;" - Acts 3:19 KJV

Prayer 75

I don't think I'm the smartest, nor do I think I'm the prettiest, but God, I know I am valuable to you. God, because I'm so precious, honored, and loved by you, you traded lives just for me. You made the ultimate sacrifice when you sent Jesus your only begotten son to die for me, God, little ole me. Who would have ever thought I meant so much to someone. Well, father, I realize I mean the world to you. Your mercy is so good Lord, you will deliver me from low self-esteem, promiscuity, hardship, trying to fit in, lying, and every other sin hidden in me. God teach me self-worth, how to love myself, but most importantly, how to love you. God, you have my attention help me to keep my mind stayed on you, which will result in me having perfect peace. In Jesus' name, I pray amen.

Bible Verses

"Others were given in exchange for you. I traded their lives for yours because you are precious to me. You are honored, and I love you." - Isaiah 43:4 NLT

"For God so loved the world, that he gave his only begotten Son, that whosoever believeth in him should not perish, but have everlasting life." - John 3:16 KJV

"But do thou for me, O God the Lord, for thy name's sake: because thy mercy is good, deliver thou me." - Psalms 109:21 KJV

"Thou wilt keep him in perfect peace, whose mind is stayed on thee: because he trusteth in thee." - Isaiah 26:3 KJV

Prayer 76

It's been a while since I spoke to you, God. I heard of you and read about you in Sunday school, but I don't know you for myself. I came from a Christian background, but here I am, empty without a relationship with you. I know the ten commandments, my parents taught me fornicators, idolaters, adulterers, effeminate, abusers, drunkards, thieves, covetous, revilers, extortioners shall not inherit the kingdom of God. I was raised right, but I decided to do my own thing. God, I wanted to test the waters have the time of my life. After my late-night visits, car visits, hotel visits, sneaking in, and out of my parents' house, I got a baby in my womb at a very young age. Some people can hide their sin, but I can't hide this baby growing in me. I'm so sorry God I failed you and stood against everything pertaining to your word. Forgive me for living a sinful life. I thank you right now for being with me, you are my Mighty Warrior who saves, you take great delight in me, in your love you no longer rebuke me, but you rejoice over me with singing. I dedicate this child in my womb to you Lord let your will be done in me and my unborn child's life in Jesus marvelous name I pray amen.

Bible Verses

9 "Know ye not that the unrighteous shall not inherit the kingdom of God? Be not deceived: neither fornicators, nor idolaters, nor adulterers, nor effeminate, nor abusers of themselves with mankind, 10 Nor thieves, nor covetous, nor drunkards, nor revilers, nor extortioners, shall inherit the kingdom of God." - 1 Corinthians 6:9-10 KJV

12 "Honour thy father and thy mother: that thy days may be long upon the land which the Lord thy God giveth thee. "13 "Thou shalt not kill." 14" Thou shalt not commit adultery." 15 " Thou shalt not steal. 16 Thou shalt not bear false witness against thy neighbour. " 17 "Thou shalt not covet thy neighbour's house, thou shalt not covet thy neighbour's wife, nor his manservant, nor his maidservant, nor his ox, nor his ass, nor any thing that is thy neighbour's." - Exodus 20:12-17 KJV

"Where is another God like you, who pardons the guilt of the remnant, overlooking the sins of his special people? You will not stay angry with your people forever, because you delight in showing unfailing love." - Micah 7:18 NLT

"For the Lord your God is living among you. He is a mighty savior. He will take delight in you with gladness. With his love, he will calm all your fears. He will rejoice over you with joyful songs." - Zephaniah 3:17

Prayer 77

God, I'm tired of being a follower. All the cool girls at school have boyfriends; some had abortions or a baby already. I want popularity; I strongly desire to fit in with my peers. I used to wear tennis shoes and jeans every day now. I wear a lot of makeup, tight skimpy clothes, and high heels. I couldn't pay boys to give me attention now; the boys are paying me for all my attention. I have a big secret I'm hiding from my parents. I'm pregnant and don't know who the father is. God, you used Rahab, a prostitute, to save the Israelites. If you did that back in the Old Testament, I know you have a plan for me. Lord, you said you know the thoughts you have towards me, thoughts of peace, and not of evil, to give me an expected end. God, I feel week and foolish, but you chose the foolish things of the world to confound the wise; you chose the weak things of the world to confound the things which are mighty. God forgive me of my sins, Jesus' blood of the New Testament was shed for the remission of sins. That's all I can say right now, but before I go, Father God, you're so beautiful. In my tears, you manage to make me smile because you love me more than a parent or a friend. God, you are always there for me even when I am disobedient. Thank you, God, for being a God who gives second chances in Jesus' name I pray amen.

Bible Verses

"So Joshua spared Rahab the prostitute and her relatives who were with her in the house, because she had hidden the spies

Joshua sent to Jericho. And she lives among the Israelites to this day." - Joshua 6:25 NLT

"For I know the thoughts that I think toward you, saith the Lord, thoughts of peace, and not of evil, to give you an expected end." - Jeremiah 29:11 KJV

"But God hath chosen the foolish things of the world to confound the wise; and God hath chosen the weak things of the world to confound the things which are mighty;"
- 1 Corinthians 1:27 KJV

"For this is my blood of the new testament, which is shed for many for the remission of sins." - Matthew 26:28 KJV

Prayer 78

Father forgive this man who stole my virginity from me, for he knows not what he does. You told me love my enemies, bless them that curse me. I want to do the opposite, but God work in my heart. I'm asking you to give me the strength to forgive this man. Thank you, Lord, I can do all things through Jesus Christ who strengthens me. Stop the vengeful desires in my heart. I will wait on you, Lord, and you will handle this matter. God bring a Holy Ghost filled man in my mother's life. Console my mama through this hard time. Let her know she didn't fail me as a parent, and I don't blame her for her boyfriend's actions. God use this situation to bring my mother and I closer. My mother shall not hate my child or me. Thank you, Lord, she knows the truth, and the truth is setting her free. Whatever I do Lord, I will do it all for the glory of God. Continue to let your unfailing love comfort me, just as you promised me your beloved daughter. God make a way out of no way for me, my mother, and my child. Please bless me with provision and satisfy my poor with bread in Jesus name I pray amen.

Bible Verses

"Then said Jesus, Father, forgive them; for they know not what they do. And they parted his raiment, and cast lots."
- Luke 23:34 KJV

"But I say unto you, Love your enemies, bless them that curse you, do good to them that hate you, and pray for them which

despitefully use you, and persecute you;" - *Matthew 5:44 KJV*

"I can do all things through Christ which strengtheneth me."
- Philippians 4:13 KJV

"Don't say, "I will get even for this wrong." Wait for the Lord
to handle the matter." - Proverbs 20:22 NLT

"Whether therefore ye eat, or drink, or whatsoever ye do, do
all to the glory of God." - 1 Corinthians 10:31 KJV

"Now let your unfailing love comfort me, just as you promised
me, your servant." - Psalms 119:76 NLT

"I will abundantly bless her provision: I will satisfy her poor
with bread." - Psalms 132:15 KJV

Prayer 79

Gracious Father, thank you for waking me up this morning. Thank you, Lord, for a new day with new mercies. God, you provide the big and small things for me. The simple fact that I didn't die in my sleep is a reason why I have to lift up my voice and give you all the praise. If I had a thousand tongues, I couldn't praise you enough. All hail King Jesus!!! You are a great God, the only mighty and awesome God. I fear you, God, and thank you in advance for delivering me out of the hands of all my enemies. People talk to me like I'm pure trash. I was sexually abused, and the father of my child isn't coming forth with the truth. I'm told to keep the identity of this man secret because I will ruin his reputation as a man of God. Father God, I ask you to expose this man right now in the name of Jesus. You said nothing is secret that shall not be made manifest. I'm going to continue to love my enemies, but God don't allow this man to get away with abusing minors. A just man falls seven times but rises up again. Father God, if this man claiming to be a man of God don't repent and turn away from his sins, let your wrath be on him for living ungodly. My enemies prepared a net for my steps; my soul is bowed down: they have dug a pit for me, but the same pit they dug for me; they fell in themselves. God, I trust you! I know me, and my baby would have the beautiful, victorious life I desire because you richly give my child and me all we need for our enjoyment. God, forgive me for my sins and transform me into the daughter of God; you predestined me to be. I will be a successful, educated, pure, and righteous mother to all my children in Jesus' noble name. I pray, amen.

Bible Verses

"For the Lord your God is the God of gods and Lord of lords. He is the great God, the mighty and awesome God, who shows no partiality and cannot be bribed." - Deuteronomy 10:17 NLT

"But the Lord your God ye shall fear; and he shall deliver you out of the hand of all your enemies." - 2 Kings 17:39 KJV

"For nothing is secret, that shall not be made manifest; neither any thing hid, that shall not be known and come abroad." - Luke 8:17 KJV

"But I say unto you which hear, Love your enemies, do good to them which hate you," - Luke 6:27 KJV

"For a just man falleth seven times, and riseth up again: but the wicked shall fall into mischief." - Proverbs 24:16 KJV

"For the wrath of God is revealed from heaven against all ungodliness and unrighteousness of men, who hold the truth in unrighteousness;" - Romans 1:18 KJV

"They have prepared a net for my steps; my soul is bowed down: they have digged a pit before me, into the midst whereof they are fallen themselves. Selah." - Psalms 57:6 KJV

"Teach those who are rich in this world not to be proud and not to trust in their money, which is so unreliable. Their trust should be in God, who richly gives us all we need for our enjoyment." - 1 Timothy 6:17 NLT

Prayer 80

God, I did the unthinkable I disobeyed you and deceived my best friend. I slept with my best friend's boyfriend, and four weeks later, I'm carrying his child. God, I was selfish when I entertained his lustful ways. I fell for a guy who doesn't love or care about me. I was a familiar friend whom she trusted, ate bread with her, just to turn around and betray her. God forgive me of my sins, I'm confessing them to you as well as turning from them. Thank you, Lord, that I have received your mercy. You are my shield, my glory, and the lifter of my head. God, I'm giving this situation to you. I decided to forget the former things, neither consider the things of the old. Yes, I was wrong, but I will not walk in guilt and shame. I will press through this situation. God touch my best friend; you change the hearts of kings; I know you are more than able to change her heart. Please, Lord let her forgive me, and if it is your will, we still be friends, then we will. I am a teen mom, but I ask you to provide, protect, and give me and my baby longevity for your word said anything I ask in your name you will do it. Also, God deliver this young man from being a two-timing, trifling charming womanizer. Lead him down the right path father God, let me my best friend and my child's father have a life-changing encounter with you in Jesus name I pray amen.

Bible Verses

"Yea, mine own familiar friend, in whom I trusted, which did

eat of my bread, hath lifted up his heel against me."
- Psalm 41:9 KJV

"People who conceal their sins will not prosper,
but if they confess and turn from them, they will receive
mercy." - Proverbs 28:13 NLT

"But thou, O Lord, art a shield for me; my glory, and the lifter
up of mine head." - Psalm 3:3 KJV

"Remember ye not the former things, neither consider the
things of old." - Isaiah 43:18 KJV

"In the first year of King Cyrus of Persia, the Lord fulfilled
the prophecy he had given through Jeremiah. He stirred the
heart of Cyrus to put this proclamation in writing and to send it
throughout his kingdom." - Ezra 1:1 NLT

"Yes, ask me for anything in my name, and I will do it!"
- John 14:14 NLT

Prayer 81

Heavenly Father, I am a straight-A student. I'm graduating top of my class. I have high test scores and several colleges that are willing to give me a shot. God, I'm pregnant, but don't let my life stop here. Lord, God, please order my steps in this pregnancy and with my education. I am like a tree planted by the rivers of water, that bringeth forth his fruit in his season; his leaf also shall not wither, and whatsoever he doeth shall prosper. Thank you, God, that I excel and prosper as your daughter, a mother, student, and a potential professional working in the workforce. Teach me how to listen to instruction, so my unborn child and I will continue to prosper. God, I want to submit to you and have peace, you will guarantee things go well for me. God, whatever I'm lacking spiritually fill that lack for me father God. God, thank you for forgiving me of current sins and my old sins. God, I want a genuine relationship with you. I have been inconsistent in the past, but God teach and show me how to be who you called me to be in your son Jesus's great name I pray amen.

Bible Verses

"And he shall be like a tree planted by the rivers of water, that bringeth forth his fruit in his season; his leaf also shall not wither; and whatsoever he doeth shall prosper." - Psalm 1:3 KJV

"Those who listen to instruction will prosper; those who trust the Lord will be joyful." - Proverbs 16:20

NLT

Submit to God, and you will have peace;
then things will go well for you." - Job 22:21 NLT

Chapter Eight

Godly Delivery

Prayer 82

God, it's almost time for me to deliver my beautiful, healthy, normal, and pure baby. Fear is trying to creep up on me, but when I am afraid, I will put my trust in you. I want a delivery different than every other delivery in this hospital. I won't curse, stress, or have a long horrifying labor. Lord, stand by me and give me the strength I need to push this baby quickly. My baby will not be breached; still, birth, suffer from neonatal death, premature death, disabilities, congenital disabilities, chromosomal issues, or any form of infirmities in Jesus's name. Before I call you God, you have answered all my prayers for my unborn child. God, your so good I will stay in the hospital for the minimum amount of days because there are no complications with my pregnancy, I and my baby are whole. I plead the blood of Jesus over all the physicians and staff members that I encounter throughout my pregnancy. Anoint their hands to do what's right, anoint their mouths to say the right things to me, father God. I ask that every test ran on me and my child come back with excellent results in your son Jesus name I pray amen.

Bible Verses

*"But when I am afraid, I will put my trust in you." -
Psalms 56:3 NLT*

"Notwithstanding the Lord stood with me and strengthened me; that by me the preaching might be fully known, and that all the Gentiles might hear, and I was delivered out of the mouth of the

lion. " - *2 Timothy 4:17 KJV*

"And it shall come to pass, that before they call, I will answer; and while they are yet speaking, I will hear." - Isaiah 65:24 KJV

Prayer 83

Time is cracking down God, but the doctor is telling me my cervix is starting to open. Father God, I rebuke every symptom in my body, leading to preterm labor. Lord close my cervix and keep it close until I'm full term. I don't come in agreement with having an incompetent cervix that can lead to miscarriages and preterm labor. Thank you, Lord, for taken sickness away from me. You have brought me health, cure my cervix, and revealed to me the abundance of peace and truth. God, it is you who blessed me with this child, and you have all the power in your hands to stop me from losing my baby. You said there will be no miscarriages or infertility in my land; you will give me a long full life. God, next time I go for a checkup, the doctor will be telling me my cervix is no longer opening. Lord, if it's your will, I take Makena shots or agree to any medical procedure to keep this baby in my womb, let your will be done. I will not have an unbearable pregnancy. The delivery of this child will be smooth sailing. The same way Jesus was whole in his mother's womb, my baby will be born whole. Thank you, Lord, for my full-term pregnancy and perfect baby you blessed me with in Jesus name I pray amen.

Bible Verses

"And ye shall serve the Lord your God, and he shall bless thy bread, and thy water; and I will take sickness away from the midst of thee." - Exodus 23:25 KJV

"Behold, I will bring it health and cure, and I will cure them,

and will reveal unto them the abundance of peace and truth."
Jeremiah 33:6 KJV

*"There will be no miscarriages or infertility in your land, and
I will give you long, full lives." - Exodus 23:26 NLT*

Prayer 84

Gracious, Holy, perfect God, I come to you with my arms high in the sky and a heart of humility. God, I don't have many family and friends, but I ask that you send the right person to be in the room with me while I deliver my child. God don't allow a negative, evil person to hold my hands or stand by my side while I deliver my baby. Thinking about delivering a baby on my own gives me anxiety, but God, you said you would keep me in perfect peace if I keep my mind stayed on you. God, I'm going to rebuke every negative thought in my head and think of everything in my life that's true, honest, just, pure, lovely, of good report, and virtue. I can never think I'm alone when father God, you are with me always. Father God, these three stages of birth (Early Labor Phase, Active Labor Phase, and Transition Phase), let them be quick, harmless, safe, and perfect delivery. I rebuke getting an emergency C section or losing my child. I'm delivering a live baby with no health, physical, mental, verbal, and intellectual issues in Jesus' name. Jesus, you're in the making people whole business; you don't even got to touch my baby and me to make us perfectly whole. All it takes is faith; the prayer of faith saves the sick, God you raise the ill and forgive any sin they committed. Thank you, God, for your presence being with me in the delivery room in Jesus perfect name I pray amen.

Bible Verses

"Thou wilt keep him in perfect peace, whose mind is stayed on

thee: because he trusteth in thee." - Isaiah 26:3 KJV

"Finally, brethren, whatsoever things are true, whatsoever things are honest, whatsoever things are just, whatsoever things are pure, whatsoever things are lovely, whatsoever things are of good report; if there be any virtue, and if there be any praise, think on these things." - Philippians 4:8 KJV

"Teaching them to observe all things whatsoever I have commanded you: and, lo, I am with you alway, even unto the end of the world. Amen." - Matthew 28:20 KJV

"And besought him that they might only touch the hem of his garment: and as many as touched were made perfectly whole." - Matthew 14:36 KJV

"And the prayer of faith shall save the sick, and the Lord shall raise him up; and if he have committed sins, they shall be forgiven him." - James 5:15 KJV

Prayer 85

Lord, in this labor room, I'm in need of guidance this is my first time having a baby. Lord guide me along the best pathway for my life. Be my advisor and continue to watch over me, oh Lord. Having a baby is a beautiful thing; this is a good and perfect gift that you sent from above. My child will not be doomed to misfortune, for me and my child are blessed by you Lord. Thank you, God, that the angel of the Lord encamps around my child and me and delivers us. I strongly doubt you would let me conceive a child just to flat out leave me in the hospital bed without your strong hand and powerful arm. I know you are real and hear me when I pray. God, I love you and place no other above you in Jesus' beautiful name I pray amen.

Bible Verses

"The Lord says, "I will guide you along the best pathway for your life. I will advise you and watch over you." - Psalms 32:8 NLT

"Every good gift and every perfect gift is from above, and cometh down from the Father of lights, with whom is no variableness, neither shadow of turning." - James 1:17 KJV

"They will not work in vain, and their children will not be doomed to misfortune. For they are people blessed by the Lord, and their children, too, will be blessed." - Isaiah 65:23 NLT

"The angel of the Lord encampeth round about them that fear

him, and delivereth them." - Psalms 34:7 KJV

"He acted with a strong hand and powerful arm. His faithful love endures forever." - Psalms 136:12 NLT

Prayer 86

God, I'm over thirty-five with no kids, but you blessed my womb, and I have conceived. I'm in the last trimester of my pregnancy, but the medical professionals still have their doubts. During most of my pregnancy, I've heard that I'm high risk. Lord, you allowed me to conceive, and you don't make any mistakes. I do not fear bad news I confidently trust you Lord to care for my unborn child and me. God, it brings me much joy when I feel my baby moving in me; my baby is truly a blessing from you. I have been trying for years, but now I'm here ready to deliver my child you ordained to be a prophet unto the nations. I read and heard stories of women dying after delivering their babies, but God you are the reason why I will not die but live after delivering my child because you said I could do all things through Jesus Christ who strengthens me. Lord, with every push, release your angels that you have given charge over me to keep me in all my ways. This delivery will be a safe delivery without complications in Jesus name I pray amen.

Bible Verses

"They do not fear bad news; they confidently trust the Lord to care for them." - Psalms 112:7 NLT

"Before I formed thee in the belly I knew thee; and before thou camest forth out of the womb I sanctified thee, and I ordained thee a prophet unto the nations." - Jeremiah 1:5 KJV

"I shall not die, but live, and declare the works of the Lord."
- Psalms 118:17 KJV

"I can do all things through Christ which strengtheneth me."
- Philippians 4:13 KJV

"For he shall give his angels charge over thee, to keep thee in all thy ways." - Psalms 91:11 KJV

Prayer 87

God, I repented for the abortions I had in my younger days, but Lord, please don't let my sinful past stop my child from living. I will not walk in fear because you haven't given me a spirit of fear but of power love and a sound mind. I dedicate my child to you, I will train up my child in the way he/she should go, and when my child is older, he/she will not depart from you. Prepare me, God, to be loving, nurturing, righteous, encouraging, and forgiving. This child is a miracle child because abortions can cause death, a damaged cervix, scarring, and infection. But God, you delivered me from all symptoms of abortion. It was so easy to pay and terminate my baby, but keeping my child is a life-changing experience. Lord, strengthen me according to your glorious power, I will have patience and long-suffering. Lord, I know I can deliver, and I will deliver this baby. You made all the delicate, inner parts of my baby's body and knit my baby together in my womb. Thank you, God, for giving me the courage to go through with my pregnancy and listening to you instead of men. I believe and receive that my labor is short, and my baby is delivered fast with no issues in Jesus name I pray amen.

Bible Verses

"For God hath not given us the spirit of fear; but of power, and of love, and of a sound mind." - 2 Timothy 1:7 KJV

"Train up a child in the way he should go: and when he is old, he will not depart from it." - Proverbs 22:6 KJV

"Strengthened with all might, according to his glorious power, unto all patience and longsuffering with joyfulness;" - Colossians 1:11 KJV

"You made all the delicate, inner parts of my body and knit me together in my mother's womb." - Psalms 139:13 NLT

Prayer 88

Lord, I will praise your name forever and ever, for you have all the wisdom and power. I know Lord, you are God and that there is none like you. God, out of all the years I've been living, nobody can out love me or out bless me the way you do. I have made countless mistakes, but your love for me has never changed. Thank you for loving me in the middle of my mess. I was pregnant before but lost the child. I pray that my baby passes through my birth canal and out of my vagina alive and whole. Lord preserve my baby and me from all evil, preserve our souls, oh Lord. God give me beauty for ashes by allowing this baby to remain in my life as healthy as can be. I know that you hear me, and whatsoever I ask, I know that I have the petition I ask of you. Thank you, Lord, for being such a mind-blowing God in Jesus lovely name I pray amen.

Bible Verses

"He said, "Praise the name of God forever and ever, for he has all wisdom and power." - Daniel 2:20 NLT

"That all the people of the earth may know that the Lord is God, and that there is none else." - 1 Kings 8:60 KJV

"The Lord shall preserve thee from all evil: he shall preserve thy soul." - Psalms 121:7 KJV

"To appoint unto them that mourn in Zion, to give unto them beauty for ashes, the oil of joy for mourning, the garment of

praise for the spirit of heaviness; that they might be called trees of righteousness, the planting of the Lord, that he might be glorified." - Isaiah 61:3 KJV

"And if we know that he hear us, whatsoever we ask, we know that we have the petitions that we desired of him." - 1 John 5:15 KJV

Prayer 89

God, I'm a teenager ready to deliver my baby, but I'm so so so scared. The doctor is saying I might need a C section I fear being cut or catching an infection. God help me to trust you with my heart, mind, body, and soul; if I trust you, I will be safe. With all these thoughts running through my mind, your comfort delights my soul, Lord. I will be saved in childbearing because I will continue in faith, charity, and holiness with sobriety. God, you are my strength and power: and made my way perfect. God, your word is building me to deliver this baby without fear. I don't care what anybody says but only what you say matters. Lord let your will be done in this delivery room with me and my Child in Jesus name I pray amen.

Bible Verses

"The fear of man bringeth a snare: but whoso putteth his trust in the Lord shall be safe." - Proverbs 29:25 KJV

"In the multitude of my thoughts within me thy comforts delight my soul." - Psalms 94:19 KJV

"Notwithstanding she shall be saved in childbearing, if they continue in faith and charity and holiness with sobriety."
- 1 Timothy 2:15 KJV

"God is my strength and power: and he maketh my way perfect." - 2 Samuel 22:33 KJV

Prayer 90

God, here I am to bless your holy name. I'm dropping in just to have intimate time with you. You are my God; early I seek you, my soul thirsts for you. God, I'm grateful I am able to hear your voice with no stipulations. Before I travail, I brought forth, before my pain came, I was delivered of a man child (son). Bless my son oh God that you blessed me with. I am strong and will not let my hands become weak; I am rewarded for going through with my pregnancy despite my thoughts of abortion. God, you are the only protector and superhero I know. Thank you, Lord, for keeping my son and me from all harm and watching over our lives. Continue to watch over us as we come and go in your son Jesus pure name, I pray amen.

Bible Verses

"O God, thou art my God; early will I seek thee: my soul thirsteth for thee, my flesh longeth for thee in a dry and thirsty land, where no water is;" - Psalms 63:1 KJV

"Before she travailed, she brought forth; before her pain came, she was delivered of a man child." - Isaiah 66:7 KJV

"Be ye strong therefore, and let not your hands be weak: for your work shall be rewarded." - 2 Chronicles 15:7 KJV

"The Lord keeps you from all harm and watches over your life. The Lord keeps watch over you as you come and go, both now and forever." - Psalms 121:7-8 NLT

Prayer 91

Thank you, God, for attending to my prayer. From the end of the earth will I cry unto thee, when my heart is overwhelmed: lead me to the rock that is higher than I. I ask you God to release my angels to move on my behalf and stop every demonic activity that was sent to stop me from delivering my baby full-term, healthy, intelligent, and perfect. Lord continue to stand by me and give me strength; because of you God, I feel like anything is possible, and with you, all things are possible. God change the minds of doctors and show them the power of prayer. I won't yell out a curse word while delivering I will yell out praise of the glory of your grace, wherein you hath made my child and I accepted in the beloved. With no uncertainty in my mind, this delivery is comfortable and joyful in Jesus's worthy name; I pray amen.

Bible Verses

"Hear my cry, O God; attend unto my prayer. From the end of the earth will I cry unto thee, when my heart is overwhelmed: lead me to the rock that is higher than I." - Psalm 61:1-2 KJV

"But the Lord stood with me and gave me strength so that I might preach the Good News in its entirety for all the Gentiles to hear. And he rescued me from certain death."
- 2 Timothy 4:17 NLT

"Jesus looked at them intently and said, "Humanly speaking, it is impossible. But with God everything is possible."

- Matthew 19:26 NLT

"To the praise of the glory of his grace, wherein he hath made us accepted in the beloved." - Ephesians 1:6 KJV

Prayer 92

God, I'm in complete shock. I carried a child full term without knowing I was pregnant. I'm about to give birth to a child I never knew I had. Lord, whatever my baby's gender is, I'm gone love every bit of my baby. My child is a gift from the Lord; being a mother to this baby is a reward from you, Lord. I haven't had a blood test done on me during this pregnancy, so I ask you, Lord, to strengthen me, help me, and continue to hold me up. In the name of Jesus. I plead the blood of Jesus over every test utilized on my child and me; the reports are all good. I declare and decree no weapon formed against my baby and me shall prosper, and every tongue that rises against us in judgment, Lord, you will condemn. Lord, I have no baby clothes, car seat, stroller, diapers, wipes, bottles, baby wash, towels, receiving blankets, and sleeping blankets, but I ask you to give me fountains of water in the valleys, fill the deserts in my life with pools of water. Stop all shortage, and lack in my life please God. You are not a man who shall lie thank you for supplying all me and my baby's needs according to your riches and glory by Christ Jesus in Jesus' name. I pray, amen.

Bible Verses

"Children are a gift from the Lord; they are a reward from him." - Psalms 127:3 NLT

"Fear thou not; for I am with thee: be not dismayed; for I am thy God: I will strengthen thee; yea, I will help thee; yea, I will

uphold thee with the right hand of my righteousness."
- Isaiah 41:10 KJV

"No weapon that is formed against thee shall prosper; and every tongue that shall rise against thee in judgment thou shalt condemn. This is the heritage of the servants of the Lord, and their righteousness is of me, saith the Lord." - Isaiah 54:17 KJV

"I will open up rivers for them on the high plateaus. I will give them fountains of water in the valleys. I will fill the desert with pools of water. Rivers fed by springs will flow across the parched ground." - Isaiah 41:18 NLT

"But my God shall supply all your need according to his riches in glory by Christ Jesus." - Philippians 4:19 KJV

Prayer 93

Lord, your name is a strong tower: the righteous run into it and are safe. I will rejoice in you Lord and praise your holy name. You have made me a mother of multiple children. I couldn't carry multiple children without you protecting me from those who are violent and are plotting against me. I cover my children and me with the blood of Jesus in Jesus' name. You have given my babies and me the power to tread over serpents and scorpions, and all the powers of the enemy, nothing by any means, will harm us. God, my delivery is safe without pregnancy complications. My babies are coming in the time you predestined them to come. All my children will be born alive, healthy, alert, intelligent, obedient, faithful, honest, humble, loving, and holy because of you God. These children in my womb that I'm about to deliver belongs to you. Have your way with them. My children will be apostles, prophets, evangelists, pastors, and teachers. Lord, my children, are doing everything you called them to do while living on this earth in Jesus righteous name I pray amen.

Bible Verses

"The name of the Lord is a strong tower: the righteous runneth into it, and is safe." - Proverbs 18:10 KJV

"May all who are godly rejoice in the Lord and praise his holy name!" - Psalms 97:12 NLT

"O Lord, keep me out of the hands of the wicked. Protect me

from those who are violent, for they are plotting against me.”
- Psalms 140:4 NLT

“Behold, I give unto you power to tread on serpents and scorpions, and over all the power of the enemy: and nothing shall by any means hurt you.” - Luke 10:19 KJV

“And he gave some, apostles; and some, prophets; and some, evangelists; and some, pastors and teachers;” - Ephesians 4:11 KJV

My Testimony

I couldn't have written a prayer book for expectant mothers without telling my story and how the power of prayer brought me through abortion, miscarriage, neonatal death, and delivery of a healthy baby boy. I stand by the word of God who the son (Jesus) sets free is free indeed (John 8:36). I could care less about how a person feels and who got something negative to say don't take it up with me take it up with God. My testimony is the reason why I was able to overcome every obstacle in my life. The word of God states, "and they overcame him by the blood of the Lamb, and by the word of their testimony: and they loved not their lives unto the death" (Revelation 12:11 KJV). Once God forgave me of my sins I committed in my life, no demon, person, or Satan himself can hold it against me. I'm free from condemnation and want everyone reading my book to be free as well.

College Years

I was having unprotected sex with my boyfriend and ended up pregnant. I was so scared to tell anyone because I had no job, my parents paid my rent, and tuition out of pocket. So, where do I get the balls to have a baby without any source of income? In my heart, I wanted to keep my baby and knew abortion was wrong, but I was so scared of people talking down on me, turning their backs on me, bringing shame to my family. I thought of all the negative but never thought about How God is a way maker and miracle worker. I went on to have an abortion but often repented for my mistake. Time went on, I was pregnant again, but this time I had the courage to tell my family and decided to keep my baby (go me)!!!! I went to my eight-week appointment the doctor said my progesterone levels were low in five days if there isn't an increase in my progesterone levels, I will have to start progesterone shots. Well, in those five days, I was traveling from Miramar, FL, back to my apartment in Orlando, FL. I was spotting all morning than I felt cramps. Within three hours, I was bleeding hard. My best friend Keldra picked me up as soon as I got in her car. I looked down in my pants and saw my baby. I was crying so hard, but in my crying, I was crying out to God. I knew what was going on with my body; I was losing another child but not by choice. In the hospital, I text my family and friends a Bible verse pertaining to King David losing his first child with Bathsheba "Then David arose from the earth, and washed, and anointed himself, and changed his apparel, and came into the house of the Lord, and worshipped: then he came to his own house; and when he required, they set bread before him, and he did eat (2 Samuel 12:20 KJV). Yes, I was heartbroken, but I magnified God's holy name, and I healed from the situation.

After graduating with my Bachelors

The night of my graduation, I and my on and off boyfriend conceived a child. It never came to my mind to have an abortion. I had someone close to me say if I were you, I would have an abortion. The father of my child wasn't a man of God or a millionaire, but he was willing to help. Daily, I was ridiculed for having him as my baby father and having a child out of wedlock. I am not a sucker, so yes, I spoke up and defended myself and the father of my child. Come on, I'm carrying his child, so why bad mouth him? I was planning my baby shower, and he ends up getting arrested for drug charges (Thank you, Jesus, for delivering me from the thugs). I went to a church play with my big sister, but my underwear and dress were wet. I had slimy discharge, which I thought was normal because my discharge increases when I am pregnant.

That night I was on the phone arguing with the father of my child. I was praying but cried myself to sleep for two hours. Soon as I fell asleep, my water broke. Me being me was willing to deliver my baby in my bed, but my sister took me to the hospital. The next day in the afternoon, I delivered my baby, but he was born sedated. My baby looked like he was sleeping peacefully. I did not have the courage to hold my son knowing within minutes he would die. My mother and sister held him and sung Christian songs to him (Thank you mommy and Sherice). Once I found out he was dead, I was crying. The nurse eventually came in and asked if she can take his body; I told her no. After a few minutes, I snapped out of it and called the nurse to take my son Carter's body. I said aloud to be absent from the body and to be present with the Lord (2 Corinthians 5:8). In my most profound darkest moments, I, as a sinner, always ran to God and used Bible verses to uplift myself. I'm telling you if you never accepted Jesus Christ as your Lord and savior today, right now is the time to do it. Accepting Jesus Christ as my Lord and Savior is the best decision I ever made in my life.

School Teacher

I had two years of teaching experience under my belt and was living my best life, okay, honey! I still prayed, went to church weekly, was an usher at my church, and tithed faithfully, but I still ended up fornicating with the father of my previous children. If you don't cut the sin from the root, it will show up again in your life. I can go weeks, months, and years without sex, but this specific person I always crawl back to. The good news is I had money saved, a steady income, and was in school getting my Master's in Educational Psychology. I was living with my sister Carissa and her husband, Dudley. They were generous to let me live with them and stack my bread.

Once I found out I was pregnant, I knew I had to move out. At six months, my teacher contract was terminated for the next school year. I told two of my best friends Keldra and Enya. I told them because they gone pray and fast on my behalf. I can call them now with a problem; they will drop what they are doing to press in God's presence with and for me. I was praying, praying, then another situation occurred because I had a history of child loss my doctor told me I have to get a cerclage (stitches to keep the cervix closed). I got the cerclage, but now the doctor told me he doesn't recommend me traveling with a cerclage. I was in the first semester of my Master's program you know your girl still took the trip to University Wisconsin Madison and completed her two weeks residency. I was praying multiple times a day watching God deliver me from fear and lies. I cramped and spotted several days while at my summer residency. Also, several days leading to my flight to Wisconsin, I was in and out of the emergency room for fake contractions. God kept me, though, and I had all the faith in the world to complete my summer residency. God supplied my needs; I had a beautiful and successful baby shower. The month before giving birth, I moved to a nice and cozy apartment with updated appliances. The same day I moved in my apartment was the same day my furniture arrived. God performed so many miracles for me; I was hired on a Saturday morning over the phone for a second-grade teacher position. I was big and pregnant hired on a weekend when teachers get hired on weekdays. God will never give up on you; if you give up on yourself, it's your personal choice. I had my son close to thirty-nine weeks, and he was perfect. My baby was so beautiful and healthy. I previously prayed Lord to show me you are real and my baby is healthy when he is delivered he is screaming and crying. God did exactly that my baby was screaming and crying; God was showing me my baby was born whole.

Single mom issues

I had money saved up, but my money was running short. The government helps depending on your income. Once my money ran up, I had my twin sister Sasha, My mommy and daddy helping me faithfully. My twin sister would cash app or Zelle me money without telling me. My mother would send thousands of dollars to pay for my son's daycare and bills. I always had financial support, and I'm grateful God blessed me with the family I got. In 2017, I lost my taxes due to a state grant that turned into a student loan because I didn't complete a specific graduate program. I called my father and asked him for $3,000.00 my daddy sent the money with no problem. My bills were paid, and I had everything I needed for my graduation. I graduated with my Master's in Educational Psychology with a 3.6 GPA (Mainly A's). I was a single mom, full-time teacher, graduate student; my family stayed an hour away. I was still able to complete my graduate program with a decent GPA look at the power of God.

God changes the heart of man

I didn't want to be with the father of my child at all; he wasn't helping, but I'm led to believe he wasn't financially stable. I made plans to move to Texas to be a teacher, but God had other plans. I miss the Texas teacher state exam by a few points, and the father of my child was taking me to court to prevent me from moving. I wasn't nasty to the father of my child or bad mouth him, but nobody wants to lose a good thing (I'm the good thing). I got a lawyer and pursued the case from that day forward, the father of my child has been helping consistently. He pays up Chase's daycare, buys him nice clothes, shoes, and toys. He also spends quality time with my son.

On the day of my court case, the father of my child called me and dropped the case against me. No matter how deep you are in a situation, God will deliver you.

Current Pregnancy

Writing this book, I'm six months pregnant with a new doctor. This doctor gave me a cerclage and weekly Makena shots. I disagree with the shots and cerclage, but doctors only practice medicine; God is the healer. I know and believe this baby will be a healthy, beautiful baby, just like my last child. My prayer is the next doctor that delivers my child don't give me shots or a cerclage, and God's name is magnified. I didn't spot or have early contractions in this pregnancy. The father of my child still helps. If I ever need money, I have my loving sister Sasha who will give me money without paying her back and my parents. I came to the point of my life; I was tired of living under the word of God. I went to God, crying and begging for a strategic mind and blueprint for my business. God gave me *Prayers for Expectant Mothers*. I never thought I would be a book author or even write a Christian prayer book. God took something I love doing prayer and used it to start my own business. I wrote all this to say God can do anything you think and dream about. Time after time, I fornicated, but he still provided, made a way, and forgave me. My son's daycare has never been late, my lights are never off, and I never had an eviction or repossession. The fact that I never lost my mind is more than enough reason to worship and serve God with everything within me.

Nosy Judgmental folks

This section is for the people who want to know how a woman who fornicated can and currently pregnant write a Christian prayer book.

Well let me nip this in the bud I decided to refrain from sex during the process of creating my book and the goal is to abstain from sex until I'm married. Instead of judging me, turn down your plate and fast for me. Everyone has sin; they deal with but the difference between me is I didn't kill my child or was using birth control. John 8: 7 "All right, but let the one who has never sinned throw the first stone!" Think about all the mistakes you made and how it felt when someone ridiculed you or threw your mistakes up in your face. You don't want it done to you, so don't do it to others.

Thank you

Sorry if I forget anyone, but I got to thank the people who always had my back. Thank you, mommy, for raising me to call on Jesus and to live righteously. When I messed up, you were there to encourage me in Christ, and you always cut the check. Daddy, thank you for showing me how to work hard to get everything I want. Daddy, you spend so much money on me; the prayer is to take care of you and mommy before you all go to be with the Lord. Thank you, Mary (Step-mom), for always being there for me financially and emotionally. Thank you, Carissa and Dudley, for opening your doors to me without treating me like a stepchild. Dudley, you took me to Memorial West to deliver my baby boy. I look up to y'all relationship. Ryan, you are one of my favorite cousins you make sure Chase got the latest Jordans. I have never gotten into an argument with you and love you like a brother. Thank you, little big cousin Okom for always cooking me the best meals and helping me around my apartment. You drove to West Palm Beach for several days to help me with infant Chase. Twiny Sasha, we are the same age, but I look up to you. You shut the lion's mouth literally when you became a lawyer.

I am grateful for all the times you sent me money without complaining and treating me beneath you. Sherice, we call and talk weekly about the things of the Lord and life. Thank you for using your PTO days to spend a week with me to take care, my newborn baby. You thought that much of me to use your PTO days on me. Tj, you are a good father to chase, and I appreciate you I can call or text you Chase wants food, this or that and you cash app the money with no problems. Thank you, Caryle, for watching Chase on weekends when I just needed a break. Thank you, Khory and Kat, for being a family for another mother. Big dawg Woody thank you for doing my make up every time I call you for a Khory Fulton photoshoot, we been down since jits! Thank you, Adrianna, Rumika, and Wytrina for believing in the calling on my life God has blessed me with. Last but not least, my two best friends and sisters in Christ: Keldra and Enya. Thank you for being a helping hand and shoulder to lean on. Big ups to you, Enya, for splitting Chase's Cuban link jewelry set with me, he wasn't even born yet but had jewelry. Enya, you read over all my prayers to make sure they were ready for the world. I text you all with my deepest darkest thoughts and feelings, knowing you won't gossip about me and spread my business. You all feel my hurt, and I feel you all hurt. It was ordained by God that we are friends (A friend loveth at all times, and a brother is born for adversity, Proverbs 17:17). Special thanks to you, everyone who has prayed for me throughout my life and will continue to pray for me. I love you all.

You don't have to wait another second to give your

life to Jesus and accept him in your heart. Here is a prayer you can pray to receive Jesus in your heart.

Sinner's Prayer

Father God, I am not perfect; I have committed sins, but I ask you to forgive me for every single sin I committed in my life. Forgive me, God, for the things in my life that's contrary to your word. Renew my mind, God, the same mind that was in Christ Jesus let it be in me. Take away every unclean in me and make me clean. I believe you are God, and the only way I can have relations with you is if I accept your only begotten son Jesus Christ as my Lord and savior.

Jesus, I believe you died on the cross for my sins and rose on the third day. Jesus, I ask you to come into my heart and never leave me or forsake me. Holy Spirit come upon me and bless me with your fruits and your gifts. Change me inside out and teach me how to be like you. You are the one true living God in your son Jesus name I pray, amen.

"Our Father" Prayer

If you don't know how to pray start with the "Our Father" Prayer
found in Matthew 6: 9-13

"After this manner, therefore, pray ye: Our Father which art in heaven, Hallowed be thy name. Thy kingdom come, thy will be done in earth, as it is in heaven. Give us this day our daily bread. And forgive us our debts, as we forgive our debtors. And lead us not into temptation but deliver us from evil: For thine is the kingdom, and the power, and the glory, forever. Amen."

Must Read
If you've had an abortion

After you have an abortion, you have come in a covenant with the evil spirit Molech. People sacrificed their children to this evil spirit "Do not permit any of your children to be offered as a sacrifice to Molech, for you must not bring shame on the name of your God. I am the Lord." This Bible verse is found in Leviticus 18:21 NLT. I want you to know as long as you are living, God will forgive you of your sins "For I will be merciful to their unrighteousness, and their sins and their iniquities will I remember no more." Hebrews 8:12 KJV.

Prayer

Father God, forgive me for opening up the door for evil spirits to have a covenant with me. Forgive me for having an abortion and sacrificing my baby to Molech. In the name of Jesus, I bleed the blood of Jesus over my womb; I rebuke the spirit of death and every spirit that's not the Holy Spirit in my life. Jesus, you disarmed the spiritual rulers and authorities. You shamed them publicly by your victory over them on the cross (Colossians 2:15 NLT). In the name of Jesus, I bleed the blood of Jesus over me and every part of my body, the blood of Jesus over my bloodline, and the generations I am going to birth out of me. I will not lose another child because my womb is a reward from the Lord (Psalm 127:3). From here on out, I am free from guilt and shame I am at peace, and now you forgave me for having an abortion. Satan can no longer hold my abortion or abortions over my head get thee behind me Satan I belong to the one true living God I'm joint-heirs with Jesus (Romans 8:17). I tear down, dismantle, uproot every assignment of the enemy in my life and family's life. Thank you, Jesus, for my healthy, whole, beautiful, intelligent, prudent children in Jesus holy and matchless name I pray amen.

Resources

Government Assistance for Mothers located in Florida

Inexpensive health insurance for kids:

https://floridakidcare.org

Food stamps, cash assistance, pregnancy Medicaid:

https://www.myflorida.com/accessflorida/

Childcare services:

https://www.flheadstart.org/

Woman, infants, and children (WIC):

http://www.floridahealth.gov/programs-and-services/wic/index.html

ABOUT THE AUTHOR

Natasha DeCruise is a native of Florida, where she currently resides. She is a skilled teacher with five years of teaching experience in South Florida. She holds a bachelors degree in Elementary Education from the University of Central Florida, and a masters degree in Educational Psychology from the University of Wisconsin-Madison, where she graduated with honors. Natasha is also a certified Christian Life/HIScoach. Above all the degrees and credentials, a relationship with Jesus Christ is most important to Natasha. Success is meaningless to her without Him.

During one of her routine nightly prayers, God deposited the idea to write a prayer book for expectant mothers in her spirit. With the power of the Holy Spirit, she completed this prayer book while working as a full-time teacher, a single parent to her handsome son, Chase Bentley, and awaiting the arrival of her new prince. Natasha wants the world to know, especially mothers, that God has a plan to prosper you and your children and not to harm you all, plans to give you and your children hope and a future. (Jeremiah 29:11).